BECKET

*is a violently emotio... ...na
that probes the c...
tionship betwee...
—between ...
bound to... ...e
of flesh... ...ome
deadly e... ...pursue
their separ... ...es ... that
of king ... a... ...nt.*

"M. Anouilh's essential theme—the portrayal of a life that ends by championing the honor of God, no matter what the cost—has nobility and exaltation."—Howard Taubman, *The New York Times*

"Fascinating play ... so much that is hopeful, stimulating, imaginatively gratifying."
—Walter Kerr
The New York Herald Tribune

Other SIGNET Plays You'll Want to Read

BECKET

or

THE HONOR OF GOD

by Jean Anouilh

Translated by *Lucienne Hill*

A SIGNET BOOK from

NEW AMERICAN LIBRARY

TIMES MIRROR

SIGNET TRADEMARK REG. U.S. PAT. OFF. AND FOREIGN COUNTRIES
REGISTERED TRADEMARK—MARCA REGISTRADA
HECHO EN CHICAGO, U.S.A.

SIGNET, SIGNET CLASSICS, SIGNETTE, MENTOR AND PLUME BOOKS
are published by The New American Library, Inc.,
1301 Avenue of the Americas, New York, New York 10019

PRINTED IN THE UNITED STATES OF AMERICA

INTRODUCTION

I am not a serious man, I wrote *Becket* by chance. I had
bought on the quays of the Seine—where, in curious little
stalls set up on the parapet, old gentlemen of another age
sell old books to other old gentlemen and to the very young
—*The Conquest of England by the Normans,* by Augustin
Thierry, an historian of the Romantic school, forgotten today and scrapped; for history, too, has its fashions.

I did not expect to read this respectable work, which
I assumed would be boring. I had bought it because it had
a pretty green binding and I needed a spot of green on my
shelves. All the same, when I returned home I skimmed
through the book (I am well-mannered with old books)
and I happened upon the chapters that tell the story of
Becket, some thirty pages, which one might have taken
to be fiction except that the bottoms of the pages were
jammed with references in Latin from the chroniclers of
the twelfth century.

I was dazzled. I had expected to find a saint—I am always a trifle distrustful of saints, as I am of great theatre
stars—and I found a man.

The idea of writing a play about it skirted my mind, as
the idea to become a fencing champion had done in my
childhood. Just as I was reminding myself that I was not a
serious man and that probably this was not for me, the tele-
phone rang. I began to exchange the latest news about a
family that held for me not the faintest glimmer of interest;
then I was told that dinner was served and at the same
time I would have to take strong measures against my son

who had just laid low both his sisters with his bare fists; I was reminded at the same time of the evening mail, which contained letters from two spongers and three actresses (the three who were miraculously destined to play all the feminine leads in my plays); then came a sinister gray envelope, a note from my tax collector . . . I completely forgot about Becket.

The following winter, green decidedly did not look well on my shelves in Paris and I bought an admirable red Balzac, first edition; I took *The Conquest of England by the Normans* to a mountain chalet where the shelves were a little empty.

One evening I was playing a game of solitaire, a game that for twenty years I have failed to bring off: my young wife, wearied by the endless spectacle of my failures, the extent of which she is only partially aware, decided to go up to bed and asked me for a book with which to read herself to sleep. I removed one of the green volumes on the shelves behind me and told her, "Read the story of Becket, it is beautiful," and I continued to fail at my solitaire, a gauge of my serenity and self-confidence. (The day that I succeed, the shock will be so great that I will probably have to be locked up in a psychiatric ward.)

An hour passed by the tick-tock of the Swiss cuckoo clock I have taught to play mischief with time; and I was in a state of remorse over that extra shot of whiskey and those last cigarettes of the day; the ones that will probably kill you in the end, which in fact no longer give you any pleasure. My wife appeared at the top of the stairs in her pajamas. She had tears in her eyes.

I was about to defend myself when I realized the tears had actually nothing to do with me. She simply told me (and I can still recall the emotion expressed in her face at that moment), "Oh, how beautiful it is! Why don't you make a play of it? It's absolutely you!"

I muttered something; I went up to bed and the next day at 8 o'clock I started, without a plan, to write the first word. Everything was marshaled in my mind. It was already written, I had only to copy it out. In fifteen happy days I finished the first part.

Then I returned to Paris, where I have never written anything, except my first play, necessitated by poverty, and that play, incidentally, provided me with the means for writing my second one in the country.

In the meantime, life went on as usual in Paris; rehearsals for another play; the doubt came back. The second part of Becket was undoable. The troubles between the Pope and the king of France; this undercurrent conflict that lasted through seven years of exile, ending in the sham reconciliation on the plain at Ferté-Bernard and finally death in the cathedral, a subject already magnificently treated by Eliot. This was certainly not for me.

The following summer, having left Paris, I started a short play, *The Fair at Empoigne,* which will be produced this winter by Jean-Louis Barrault. I completed it very easily. I felt myself in good form, my appetite whetted rather than satiated by the work. Talent is like a faucet; while it is open, one must write. Inspiration is a farce that poets have invented to give themselves importance. It was still only the middle of the summer and it was absolutely necessary that I write something else.

My wife reappeared, this time smiling, on the threshold of the bottom of the garden of a house we had rented on a beach in the Landes. She said to me simply but firmly: "You are ridiculous; finish *Becket.*"

I have always feared ridicule; and for this specific reason and, incidentally, to please her, I started the very next day on the second part of the play, a scene with some facile comedy lines that I habitually write to give myself courage and to prove to myself that the work is, after all, not as important as one would like to pretend. Things fell into their place of themselves, and in fifteen days I finished *Becket.*

Altogether shamefaced at the idea of having written an historical play, I gave it to an historian friend of mine to read, and he roared with laughter, saying: "Are you unaware that history, like everything else on this earth, makes progress? In Augustin Thierry's time one could believe that Becket was of Saxon origin; but for over fifty years we have had proof that he was a good Norman. He was from the vicinity of Rouen and was in fact called Bequet."

A large part of the subject of my play was based on the fact that Becket was of the vanquished race. A serious man at this point would have torn out his hair; then he would have rewritten his play on a more exact historical basis.

I decided that if history in the next fifty years should go on making progress it will perhaps rediscover that Becket was indubitably of Saxon origin; in any case, for this drama of friendship between two men, between the king and his friend, his companion in pleasure and in work (and this is what had gripped me about the story), this friend whom he could not cease to love though he became his worst enemy the night he was named archbishop—for this drama it was a thousand times better that Becket remained a Saxon.

I changed nothing; I had the play performed three months later in Paris. It had a great success and I noticed that no one except my historian friend was aware of the progress of history.

All this was part and parcel of my increasingly involved technique for unsuccessful solitaire, which has been protecting me for close to thirty years against the extreme hazards of this profession.

Jean Anouilh

Becket
opened in New York,
October 5, 1960,
at the St. James
Theatre with
the following
cast:

CHARACTERS
(In order of appearance)

Henry II	*Anthony Quinn*
Thomas Becket	*Laurence Olivier*
Archbishop of Canterbury	*Sydney Walker*
Gilbert Folliot	*Earl Montgomery*
Bishop of York	*Victor Thorley*
Saxon Peasant	*Robert Weil*
His Son	*Tom Leith*
Gwendolen	*Drani Seitz*
1st English Baron	*Louis Zorich*
2nd English Baron	*Ronald Weyand*
3rd English Baron	*Mel Berger*
4th English Baron	*Ferdi Hoffman*
Queen Mother	*Marie Powers*
The Queen	*Margaret Hall*
Louis, King of France	*Robert Eckles*
The Pope	*Edward Atienza*

Becket *was presented by David Merrick*
Directed by Peter Glenville
Settings by Oliver Smith
Costumes by Motley

ACT ONE

*An indeterminate set, with pillars. We are in
the cathedral. Center stage:* BECKET's *tomb; a
stone slab with a name carved on it. Two*
SENTRIES *come in and take up their position upstage. Then the* KING *enters from the back. He
is wearing his crown, and is naked under a big
cloak. A* PAGE *follows at a distance. The* KING
*hesitates a moment before the tomb; then re-
moves his cloak with a swift movement and the*
PAGE *takes it away. He falls to his knees on the
stone floor and prays, alone, naked, in the middle of the stage. Behind the pillars, in the shadows, one senses the disquieting presence of un-
seen lookers-on.*

KING. Well, Thomas Becket, are you satisfied? I am naked at your tomb and your monks are coming to flog me. What an end to our story! You, rotting in this tomb, larded with my barons' dagger thrusts, and I, naked, shivering in the draughts, and waiting like an idiot for those brutes to come and thrash me. Don't you think we'd have done better to understand each other?

>BECKET *in his Archbishop's robes, just as he was on the day of his death, has appeared on the side of the stage, from behind a pillar. He says softly:*

BECKET. Understand each other? It wasn't possible.

KING. I said, "In all save the honor of the realm." It was you who taught me that slogan, after all.

BECKET. I answered you, "In all save the honor of God." We were like two deaf men talking.

KING. How cold it was on that bare plain at La Ferté-Bernard, the last time we two met! It's funny, it's always been cold, in our story. Save at the beginning, when we were friends. We had a few fine summer evenings together, with the girls . . .

>*He says suddenly:*

Did you love Gwendolen, Archbishop? Did you hate me, that night when I said, "I am the King," and took her from you? Perhaps that's what you never could forgive me for?

BECKET. (*Quietly*) I've forgotten.

KING. Yet we were like two brothers, weren't we—you and I? That night it was a childish prank—a lusty lad shouting "I am the King!" . . . I was so young . . . And every thought in my head came from you, you know that.

BECKET. (*Gently, as if to a little boy*) Pray, Henry, and don't talk so much.

KING. (*Irritably*) If you think I'm in the mood for praying at the moment . . .

      BECKET *quietly withdraws into the darkness and disappears during the* KING's *next speech.*

I can see them through my fingers, spying on me from the aisles. Say what you like, they're an oafish lot, those Saxons of yours! To give oneself over naked to those ruffians! With my delicate skin . . . Even you'd be afraid. Besides, I'm ashamed. Ashamed of this whole masquerade. I need them though, that's the trouble. I have to rally them to my cause, against my son, who'll gobble up my kingdom if I let him. So I've come to make my peace with their Saint. You must admit it's funny. You've become a Saint and here am I, the King, desperately in need of that great amorphous mass which could do nothing, up till now, save lie inert beneath its own enormous weight, cowering under blows, and which is all-powerful now. What use are conquests, when you stop to think? They are England now, because of their vast numbers, and the rate at which they breed—like rabbits, to make good the massacres. But one must always pay the price—that's another thing you taught me, Thomas Becket, when you were still advising me . . . You taught me everything . . . (*Dreamily*) Ah, those were happy times . . . At the peep of dawn—well, our dawn that is, around noon, because we always went to bed very late—you'd come into my room, as I was emerging from the bathhouse, rested, smiling, debonair, as fresh as if we'd never spent the entire night drinking and whoring through the town.

He says a little sourly:

That's another thing you were better at than me . . .

      The PAGE *has come in. He wraps a white towel around the* KING *and proceeds to rub him down. Off stage is heard for the first time—we will hear it often—the gay, ironical Scottish marching song which* BECKET *is always whistling.*

      The lighting changes. We are still in the empty cathedral. Then, a moment or so later, BECKET *will draw aside a curtain and reveal the* KING's *room.*

Their manner, his and the KING'S, *faraway at first,
like a memory relived, will gradually become more
real.*
THOMAS BECKET, *dressed as a nobleman, elegant,
young, charming, in his short doublet and pointed,
upturned shoes, comes in blithely and greets the*
KING.

BECKET. My respects, my Lord!

KING. (*His face brightening*) Oh, Thomas . . . I thought
you were still asleep.

BECKET. I've already been for a short gallop to Richmond
and back, my Lord. There's a divine nip in the air.

KING. (*His teeth chattering*) To think you actually like
the cold! (*To the* PAGE) Rub harder, pig!
    Smiling, BECKET *pushes the* PAGE *aside and pro-
    ceeds to rub the* KING *himself.*

(*To the* PAGE) Throw a log on the fire and get out.
Come back and dress me later.

BECKET. My prince, I shall dress you myself.
    The PAGE *goes.*

KING. Nobody rubs me down the way you do. Thomas,
what would I do without you? You're a nobleman,
why do you play at being my valet? If I asked my
barons to do this, they'd start a civil war!

BECKET. (*Smiling*) They'll come round to it in time,
when Kings have learnt to play their role. I am your
servant, my prince, that's all. Helping you to govern
or helping you get warm again is part of the same
thing to me. I like helping you.

KING. (*With an affectionate little gesture*) My little
Saxon! At the beginning, when I told them I was taking
you into my service, do you know what they all said?

They said you'd seize the chance to knife me in the back one day.

BECKET. (*Smiling as he dresses him*) Did you believe them, my prince?

KING. N . . . no. I was a bit scared at first. You know I scare easily . . . But you looked so well brought up, beside those brutes. However did you come to speak French without a trace of an English accent?

BECKET. My parents were able to keep their lands by agreeing to "collaborate," as they say, with the King your father. They sent me to France as a boy to acquire a good French accent.

KING. To France? Not to Normandy?

BECKET. (*Still smiling*) That was their one patriotic conceit. They loathed the Norman accent.

KING. (*Distinctly*) Only the accent?

BECKET. (*Lightly and inscrutably*) My father was a very severe man. I would never have taken the liberty of questioning him on his personal convictions while he was alive. And his death shed no light on them, naturally. He managed, by collaborating, to amass a considerable fortune. As he was also a man of rigid principles, I imagine he contrived to do it in accordance with his conscience. That's a little piece of sleight of hand that men of principle are very skillful at in troubled times.

KING. And you?

BECKET. (*Feigning not to understand the question*) I, my Lord?

KING. (*Putting a touch of contempt into his voice, for despite his admiration for Thomas or perhaps because of it, he would like to score a point against him oc-*

casionally) The sleight of hand, were you adept at it too?

BECKET. (*Still smiling*) Mine was a different problem. I was a frivolous man, you'll agree? In fact, it never came up at all. I adore hunting and only the Normans and their protégés had the right to hunt. I adore luxury and luxury was Norman. I adore life and the Saxons' only birthright was slaughter. I'll add that I adore honor.

KING. (*With faint surprise*) And was honor reconciled with collaboration too?

BECKET. (*Lightly*) I had the right to draw my sword against the first Norman nobleman who tried to lay hands on my sister. I killed him in single combat. It's a detail, but it has its points.

KING. (*A little slyly*) You could always have slit his throat and fled into the forest, as so many did.

BECKET. That would have been uncomfortable, and not a lot of use. My sister would immediately have been raped by some other Norman baron, like all the Saxon girls. Today, she is respected. (*Lightly*) My Lord, did I tell you?—My new gold dishes have arrived from Florence. Will my Liege do me the honor of christening them with me at my house?

KING. Gold dishes! You lunatic!

BECKET. I'm setting a new fashion.

KING. I'm your King and I eat off silver!

BECKET. My prince, your expenses are heavy and I have only my pleasures to pay for. The trouble is I'm told they scratch easily. Still, we'll see. I received two forks as well—

KING. Forks?

BECKET. Yes. It's a new instrument, a devilish little
thing to look at—and to use too. It's for pronging
meat with and carrying it to your mouth. It saves you
dirtying your fingers.

KING. But then you dirty the fork?

BECKET. Yes. But it's washable.

KING. So are your fingers. I don't see the point.

BECKET. It hasn't any, practically speaking. But it's re-
fined, it's subtle. It's very un-Norman.

KING. (*With sudden delight*) You must order me a
dozen! I want to see my great fat barons' faces, at the
first court banquet, when I present them with that! We
won't tell them what they're for. We'll have no end of
fun with them.

BECKET. (*Laughing*) A dozen! Easy now, my Lord! Forks
are very expensive you know! My prince, it's time for
the Privy Council.

KING. (*Laughing too*) They won't make head nor tail of
them! I bet you they'll think they're a new kind of
dagger. We'll have a hilarious time!
> *They go out, laughing, behind the curtain, which
> draws apart to reveal the same set, with the pil-
> lars. The Council Chamber. The Councilors stand
> waiting. The* KING *and* BECKET *come in, still
> laughing.*

KING. (*Sitting in a chair*) Gentlemen, the Council is
open. I have summoned you here today to deal with
this refusal of the clergy to pay the absentee tax.
We really must come to an understanding about who
rules this kingdom, the Church—
> *The* ARCHBISHOP *tries to speak.*

just a moment, Archbishop!—or me! But before we quarrel, let us take the good news first. I have decided to revive the office of Chancellor of England, keeper of the Triple Lion Seal, and to entrust it to my loyal servant and subject Thomas Becket.

BECKET *rises in surprise, the color draining from his face.*

BECKET. My Lord . . . !

KING. (*Roguishly*) What's the matter, Becket? Do you want to go and piss already? True, we both had gallons to drink last night!
He looks at him with delight.
Well, that's good! I've managed to surprise you for once, little Saxon.

BECKET. (*Dropping on one knee, says gravely*) My Liege, this is a token of your confidence of which I fear I may not be worthy. I am very young, frivolous perhaps—

KING. I'm young too. And you know more than all of us put together. (*To the others*) He's read books, you know. It's amazing the amount he knows. He'll checkmate the lot of you! Even the Archbishop! As for his frivolity, don't let him fool you! He drinks strong wine, he likes to enjoy himself, but he's a lad who thinks every minute of the time! Sometimes it embarrasses me to feel him thinking away beside me. Get up, Thomas. I never did anything without your advice anyway. Nobody knew it, now everybody will, that's all.
He bursts out laughing, pulls something out of his pocket and gives it to BECKET.
There. That's the Seal. Don't lose it. Without the Seal, there's no more England and we'll all have to go back to Normandy. Now, to work!
The ARCHBISHOP *rises, all smiles, now the first shock is over.*

ARCHBISHOP. May I crave permission to salute, with my Lord's approval, my young and learned archdeacon here? For I was the first—I am weak enough to be proud of pointing it out—to notice him and take him under my wing. The presence at this Council, with the preponderant title of Chancellor of England, of one of our brethren—our spiritual son in a sense—is a guarantee for the Church of this country, that a new era of agreement and mutual understanding is dawning for us all and we must now, in a spirit of confident cooperation—

KING. (*Interrupting*) Etc., etc. . . . Thank you, Archbishop! I knew this nomination would please you. But don't rely too much on Becket to play your game. He is my man.

    He turns to BECKET, *beaming.*

Come to think of it, I'd forgotten you were a deacon, little Saxon.

BECKET. (*Smiling*) So had I, my prince.

KING. Tell me—I'm not talking about wenching, that's a venial sin—but on the odd occasions when I've seen you fighting, it seems to me you have a mighty powerful sword arm, for a priest! How do you reconcile that with the Church's commandment forbidding a priest to shed blood?

BISHOP OF OXFORD. (*Prudently*) Our young friend is only a deacon, he has not yet taken all his vows, my Lord. The Church in its wisdom knows that youth must have its day and that—under the sacred pretext of a war— a holy war, I mean, of course, young men are permitted to—

KING. (*Interrupting*) All wars are holy wars, Bishop! I defy you to find me a serious belligerent who doesn't have Heaven on his side, in theory. Let's get back to the point.

ARCHBISHOP. By all means, your Highness.

KING. Our customs demand that every landowner with
sufficient acreage to maintain one must send a man-
at-arms to the quarterly review of troops, fully armed
and shield in hand, or pay a tax in silver. Where is
my tax?

BISHOP OF OXFORD. *Distingo,* your Highness.

KING. Distinguish as much as you like. I've made up my
mind. I want my money. My purse is open, just drop
it in.
> *He sprawls back in his chair and picks his teeth.*
> *To* BECKET.

Thomas, I don't know about you, but I'm starving.
Have them bring us something to eat.
> BECKET *makes a sign to the* SENTRY *who goes out.*
> *A pause. The* ARCHBISHOP *rises.*

ARCHBISHOP. A layman who shirks his duty to the State,
which is to assist his Prince with arms, should pay the
tax. Nobody will question that.

KING. (*Jovially*) Least of all the clergy!

ARCHBISHOP. (*Continuing*) A churchman's duty to the
State is to assist his Prince in his prayers, and in his
educational and charitable enterprises. He cannot
therefore be liable to such a tax unless he neglects
those duties.

BISHOP OF OXFORD. Have we refused to pray?

KING. (*Rising in fury*) Gentlemen! Do you seriously
think that I am going to let myself be swindled out of
more than two thirds of my revenues with arguments
of that sort? In the days of the Conquest, when there
was booty to be had, our Norman abbots tucked up
their robes all right. And lustily too! Sword in fist,
hams in the saddle, at cockcrow or earlier! "Let's go
to it, Sire! Out with the Saxon scum! It's God's will!

It's God's will!" You had to hold them back then! And on the odd occasions when you wanted a little Mass, they never had the time. They'd mislaid their vestments, the churches weren't equipped—any excuse to put it off, for fear they'd miss some of the pickings while their backs were turned!

ARCHBISHOP. Those heroic days are over. It is peacetime now.

KING. Then pay up! I won't budge from that.
Turning to BECKET.
Come on, Chancellor, say something! Has your new title caught your tongue?

BECKET. May I respectfully draw my Lord Archbishop's attention to one small point?

KING. (*Grunting*) Respectfully, but firmly. You're the Chancellor now.

BECKET. (*Calmly and casually*) England is a ship.

KING. (*Beaming*) Why, that's neat! We must use that, sometime.

BECKET. In the hazards of seafaring, the instinct of self-preservation has always told men that there must be one and only one master on board ship. Mutinous crews who drown their captain always end up, after a short interval of anarchy, by entrusting themselves body and soul to one of their number, who then proceeds to rule over them, more harshly sometimes than their drowned captain.

ARCHBISHOP. My Lord Chancellor—my young friend—there is in fact a saying—the captain is sole master after God.
He thunders suddenly, with a voice one did not suspect from that frail body:
After God!

He crosses himself. All the BISHOPS *follow suit.
The wind of excommunication shivers through the
Council. The* KING, *awed, crosses himself too and
mumbles, a little cravenly.*

KING. Nobody's trying to question God's authority, Archbishop.

BECKET. (*Who alone has remained unperturbed*) God
steers the ship by inspiring the captain's decisions. But
I never heard tell that He gave His instructions directly to the helmsman.
    GILBERT FOLLIOT, *Bishop of London, rises. He is
a thin-lipped, venomous man.*

FOLLIOT. Our young Chancellor is only a deacon—but
he is a member of the Church. The few years he has
spent out in the tumult of the world cannot have
made him forget so soon that it is through His Church
Militant and more particularly through the inter-
mediary of our Holy Father the Pope and his Bishops
—his qualified representatives—that God dictates His
decisions to men!

BECKET. There is a chaplain on board every ship, but he
is not required to determine the size of the crew's ra-
tions, nor to take the vessel's bearings. My Reverend
Lord the Bishop of London—who is the grandson of
a sailor they tell me—cannot have forgotten that point
either.

FOLLIOT. (*Yelping*) I will not allow personal insinua-
tions to compromise the dignity of a debate of this
importance! The integrity and honor of the Church of
England are at stake!

KING. (*Cheerfully*) No big words, Bishop. You know as
well as I do that all that's at stake is its money. I need
money for my wars. Will the Church give me any, yes
or no?

ARCHBISHOP. (*Cautiously*) The Church of England has always acknowledged that it was its duty to assist the
King, to the best of its ability, in all his needs.

KING. There's a fine speech. But I don't like the past
tense, Archbishop. There's something so nostalgic
about it. I like the present. And the future. Are you
going to pay up?

ARCHBISHOP. Your Highness, I am here to defend the
privileges which your illustrious forefather William
granted to the Church of England. Would you have the
heart to tamper with your forefather's work?

KING. May he rest in peace. His work is inviolable. But
where he is now he doesn't need money. I'm still on
earth unfortunately, and I do.

FOLLIOT. Your Highness, this is a question of principle!

KING. I'm levying troops, Bishop! I have sent for 1,500
German foot soldiers, and three thousand Swiss infan-
try to help fight the King of France. And nobody has
ever paid the Swiss with principles.

BECKET. (*Rises suddenly and says incisively*) I think,
your Highness, that it is pointless to pursue a discus-
sion in which neither speaker is listening to the other.
The law and custom of the land give us the means of
coercion. We will use them.

FOLLIOT. (*Beside himself*) Would you dare—you whom
she raised from the obscurity of your base origins—
to plunge a dagger in the bosom of your Mother
Church?

BECKET. My Lord and King has given me his Seal with
the Three Lions to guard. My mother is England now.

FOLLIOT. (*Frothing, and slightly ridiculous*) A deacon! A

miserable deacon nourished in our bosom! Traitor! Little viper! Libertine! Sycophant! Saxon!

KING. My Reverend friend, I suggest you respect my Chancellor, or else I'll call my guards.

> *He has raised his voice a little toward the end of this speech. The* GUARDS *come in.*

(*Surprised*) Why, here they are! Oh, no, it's my snack. Excuse me, gentlemen, but around noon I need something to peck at or I tend to feel weak. And a King has no right to weaken, I needn't tell you that. I'll have it in my chapel, then I can pray directly afterwards. Come and sit with me, son.

> *He goes out taking* BECKET *with him. The three prelates have risen, deeply offended. They move away, murmuring to one another, with sidelong glances in the direction in which the* KING *went out.*

FOLLIOT. We must appeal to Rome! We must take a firm line!

YORK. My Lord Archbishop, you are the Primate of England. Your person is inviolate and your decisions on all matters affecting the Church are law in this country. You have a weapon against such intransigence: excommunication.

BISHOP OF OXFORD. We must not use it save with a great deal of prudence, Reverend Bishop. The Church has always triumphed over the centuries, but it has triumphed prudently. Let us bide our time. The King's rages are terrible, but they don't last. They are fires of straw.

FOLLIOT. The little self-seeker he has at his elbow now will make it his business to kindle them. And I think, like the Reverend Bishop, that only the excommunication of that young libertine can reduce him to impotence.

> BECKET *comes in.*

BECKET. My Lords, the King has decided to adjourn his Privy Council. He thinks that a night of meditation will inspire your Lordships with a wise and equitable solution——which he authorizes you to come and submit to him tomorrow.

FOLLIOT. (*With a bitter laugh*) You mean it's time for the hunt.

BECKET. (*Smiling*) Yes, my Lord Bishop, to be perfectly frank with you, it is. Believe me, I am personally most grieved at this difference of opinion and the brutal form it has taken. But I cannot go back on what I said as Chancellor of England. We are all bound, laymen as well as priests, by the same feudal oath we took to the King as our Lord and Sovereign: the oath to preserve his life, limbs, dignity and honor. None of you, I think, has forgotten the words of that oath?

ARCHBISHOP. (*Quietly*) We have not forgotten it, my son. No more than the other oath we took, before that——the oath to God. You are young, and still uncertain of yourself, perhaps. Yet you have, in those few words, taken a resolution the meaning of which has not escaped me. Will you allow an old man, who is very close to death, and who, in this rather sordid argument, was defending more perhaps than you suspect——to hope, as a father, that you will never know the bitterness of realizing, one day, that you made a mistake.
      He holds out his ring and BECKET *kisses it.*
I give you my blessing, my son.
      BECKET *has knelt. Now he rises and says lightly:*

BECKET. An unworthy son, Father, alas. But when is one worthy? And worthy of what?
      He pirouettes and goes out, insolent and graceful as a young boy.

FOLLIOT. (*Violently*) Such insults to your Grace cannot

be tolerated! This young rake's impudence must be crushed!

ARCHBISHOP. (*Thoughtfully*) He was with me for a long time. His is a strange, elusive nature. Don't imagine he is the ordinary libertine that outward appearances would suggest. I've had plenty of opportunity to observe him, in the bustle of pleasure and daily living. He is as it were detached. As if seeking his real self.

FOLLIOT. Break him, my Lord, before he finds it! Or the clergy of this country will pay dearly.

ARCHBISHOP. We must be very circumspect. It is our task to see into the hearts of men. And I am not sure that this one will always be our enemy.

> The ARCHBISHOP *and the three* BISHOPS *go out. The* KING *is heard calling off stage.*

KING. Well, son, have they gone? Are you coming hunting?

> *Trees come down from the flies. The black velvet curtain at the back opens on a clear sky, transforming the pillars into the leafless trees of a forest in winter. Bugles. The lights have gone down. When they go up again, the* KING *and* BECKET *are on horseback, each with a hawk on his gauntleted wrist. Torrential rain is heard.*

KING. Here comes the deluge. (*Unexpectedly*) Do you like hunting this way, with hawks?

BECKET. I don't much care to delegate my errands. I prefer to feel a wild boar on the end of my spear. When he turns and charges there's a moment of delicious personal contact when one feels, at last, responsible for oneself.

KING. It's odd, this craving for danger. Why are you all so hell-bent on risking your necks for the most futile reasons?

BECKET. One has to gamble with one's life to feel alive.

KING. Or dead! You make me laugh.
    To his hawk:
Quiet, my pretty, quiet! We'll take your hood off in a
minute. You couldn't give much of a performance
under all these trees. I'll tell you one creature that
loves hawking anyway, and that's a hawk! It seems to
me we've rubbed our backsides sore with three hours'
riding, just to give them this royal pleasure.

BECKET. (*Smiling*) My Lord, these are Norman hawks.
They belong to the master race. They have a right to it.

KING. (*Suddenly, as he reins his horse*) Do you love me,
Becket?

BECKET. I am your servant, my prince.

KING. Did you love me when I made you Chancellor? I
wonder sometimes if you're capable of love. Do you
love Gwendolen?

BECKET. She is my mistress, my prince.

KING. Why do you put labels onto everything to justify
your feelings?

BECKET. Because, without labels, the world would have
no shape, my prince.

KING. Is it so important for the world to have a shape?

BECKET. It's essential, my prince, otherwise we can't
know what we're doing.
    Bugles in the distance.
The rain is getting heavier, my Lord! Come, let us shel-
ter in that hut over there.
    *He gallops off. After a second of confused in-
    decision, the* KING *gallops after him, holding his
    hawk high and shouting:*

KING. Becket! You didn't answer my question!

> *He disappears into the forest. Bugles again. The four* BARONS *cross the stage, galloping after them, and vanish into the forest. Thunder. Lightning. A hut has appeared to one side of the stage.* BECKET *is heard shouting:*

BECKET. Hey there! You! Fellow! Can we put the horses under cover in your barn? Do you know how to rub down a horse? And have a look at the right forefoot of messire's horse. I think the shoe is loose. We'll sit out the storm under your roof.

> *After a second, the* KING *enters the hut, followed by a hairy Saxon who, cap in hand, bows repeatedly, in terrified silence.*

KING. (*Shaking himself*) What a soaking! I'll catch my death!

> *He sneezes.*

All this just to keep the hawks amused!

> *Shouting at the man:*

What are you waiting for? Light a fire, dog! It's freezing cold in this shack.

> *The* MAN, *terror-stricken, does not move. The* KING *sneezes again. To* BECKET:

What is he waiting for?

BECKET. Wood is scarce, my Lord. I don't suppose he has any left.

KING. What—in the middle of the forest?

BECKET. They are entitled to two measures of dead wood. One branch more and they're hanged.

KING. (*Astounded*) Really? And yet people are always complaining about the amount of dead wood in the forests. Still, that's a problem for my intendants, not me.

> *Shouting at the* MAN:

Run and pick up all the wood you can carry and build

us a roaring fire! We won't hang you this time, dog!
The peasant, terrified, dares not obey. BECKET
says gently:

BECKET. Go, my son. Your King commands it. You've the right.
The MAN *goes out, trembling, bowing to the ground, repeatedly.*

KING. Why do you call that old man your son?

BECKET. Why not? You call him dog, my prince.

KING. It's a manner of speaking. Saxons are always called "dog." I can't think why, really. One could just as well have called them "Saxon"! But that smelly old ragbag your son!
Sniffing.
What on earth can they eat to make the place stink so—dung?

BECKET. Turnips.

KING. Turnips—what are they?

BECKET. Roots.

KING. (*Amused*) Do they eat roots?

BECKET. Those who live in the forests can't grow anything else.

KING. Why don't they move out into the open country then?

BECKET. They would be hanged if they left their area.

KING. Oh, I see. Mark you, that must make life a lot simpler, if you know you'll be hanged at the least show of initiative. You must ask yourself far fewer questions.

They don't know their luck! But you still haven't told me why you called the fellow your son?

BECKET. (*Lightly*) My prince, he is so poor and so bereft and I am so strong beside him, that he really is my son.

KING. We'd go a long way with that theory!

BECKET. Besides, my prince, you're appreciably younger than I am and you call me "son" sometimes.

KING. That's got nothing to do with it. It's because I love you.

BECKET. You are our King. We are all your sons and in your hands.

KING. What, Saxons too?

BECKET. (*Lightly, as he strips off his gloves*) England will be fully built, my prince, on the day the Saxons are your sons as well.

KING. You are a bore today! I get the feeling that I'm listening to the Archbishop. And I'm dying of thirst. Hunt around and see if you can't find us something to drink. Go on, it's your son's house!

> BECKET *starts looking, and leaves the room after a while. The* KING *looks around too, examining the hut with curiosity, touching things with grimaces of distaste. Suddenly he notices a kind of trap door at the foot of a wall. He opens it, thrusts his hand in and pulls out a terrified* GIRL. *He shouts:*

Hey, Thomas! Thomas!

> BECKET *comes in.*

BECKET. Have you found something to drink, Lord?

KING. (*Holding the* GIRL *at arm's length*) No. Something to eat. What do you say to that, if it's cleaned up a bit?

BECKET. (*Coldly*) She's pretty.

KING. She stinks a bit, but we could wash her. Look, did
you ever see anything so tiny? How old would you
say it was—fifteen, sixteen?

BECKET. (*Quietly*) It can talk, my Lord.
> *Gently, to the* GIRL:
How old are you?
> *The* GIRL *looks at them in terror and says nothing.*

KING. You see? Of course it can't talk!
> *The* MAN *has come back with the wood and stops
> in the doorway, terrified.*
How old is your daughter, dog?
> *The* MAN *trembles like a cornered animal and says
> nothing.*
He's dumb as well, that son of yours. How did you
get him—with a deaf girl? It's funny the amount of
dumb people I meet the second I set foot out of my
palace. I rule over a kingdom of the dumb. Can you tell
me why?

BECKET. They're afraid, my prince.

KING. I know that. And a good thing too. The populace
must live in fear, it's essential. The moment they stop
being afraid they have only one thought in mind—to
frighten other people instead. And they adore doing
that! Just as much as we do! Give them a chance
to do it and they catch up fast, those sons of yours!
Did you never see a peasants' revolt? I did once, in my
father's reign, when I was a child. It's not a pretty
sight.
> *He looks at the* MAN, *exasperated.*
Look at it, will you? It's tongue-tied, it's obtuse, it
stinks and the country is crawling with them!
> *He seizes the* GIRL *who was trying to run away.*
Stay here, you!
> *To* BECKET:
I ask you, what use is it?

BECKET. (*Smiling*) It scratches the soil, it makes bread.

KING. Pooh, the English eat so little of it . . . At the French Court, yes, I daresay—they fairly stuff it down! But here!

BECKET. (*Smiling*) The troops have to be fed. For a King without troops . . .

KING. (*Struck by this*) True enough! Yes, that makes sense. There must be some sort of reason in all these absurdities. Well well, you little Saxon philosopher, you! I don't know how you do it, but you'll turn me into an intelligent man yet! The odd thing is, it's so ugly and yet it makes such pretty daughters. How do you explain that, you who can explain it all?

BECKET. At twenty, before he lost his teeth and took on that indeterminate age the common people have, that man may have been handsome. He may have had one night of love, one minute when he too was a King, and shed his fear. Afterwards, his pauper's life went on, eternally the same. And he and his wife no doubt forgot it all. But the seed was sown.

KING. (*Dreamily*) You have such a way of telling things . . .
    He looks at the GIRL.
Do you think she'll grow ugly too?

BECKET. For sure.

KING. If we made her a whore and kept her at the palace, would she stay pretty?

BECKET. Perhaps.

KING. Then we'd be doing her a service, don't you think?

BECKET. (*Coldly*) No doubt.
    The MAN *stiffens. The* GIRL *cowers, in terror. The*

BROTHER *comes in, somber-faced, silent, threatening.*

KING. Would you believe it? They understand every word, you know! Who's that one there?

BECKET. (*Taking in the situation at a glance*) The brother.

KING. How do you know?

BECKET. Instinct, my Lord.
His hand moves to his dagger.

KING. (*Bawling suddenly*) Why are they staring at me like that? I've had enough of this! I told you to get something to drink, dog!
Terrified, the MAN *scuttles off.*

BECKET. Their water will be brackish. I have a gourd of juniper juice in my saddlebag. (*To the* BROTHER) Come and give me a hand, you! My horse is restive.
He seizes the boy roughly by the arm and hustles him out into the forest, carelessly whistling his little marching song. Then, all of a sudden, he hurls himself onto him. A short silent struggle. BECKET *gets the boy's knife away; he escapes into the forest.* BECKET *watches him go for a second, holding his wounded hand. Then he walks around the back of the hut. The* KING *has settled himself on a bench, with his feet up on another, whistling to himself. He lifts the* GIRL's *skirts with his cane and examines her at leisure.*

KING. (*In a murmur*) All my sons! . . .
He shakes himself.
That Becket! He wears me out. He keeps making me think! I'm sure it's bad for the health.
He gets up, BECKET *comes in followed by the* MAN. What about that water? How much longer do I have to wait?

BECKET. Here it is, my Lord. But it's muddy. Have some of this juniper juice instead.

KING. Drink with me.
> He notices BECKET's hand, wrapped in a blood-stained cloth.

What's the matter? You're wounded!

BECKET. (*Hiding his hand*) No doubt about it, that horse of mine is a nervous brute. He can't bear his saddle touched. He bit me.

KING. (*With a hearty, delighted laugh*) That's funny! Oh, that's very funny! Milord is the best rider in the Kingdom! Milord can never find a stallion with enough spirit for him! Milord makes us all look silly at the jousts, with his fancy horsemanship, and when he goes to open his saddlebags he gets himself bitten! Like a page!
> He is almost savagely gleeful. Then suddenly, his gaze softens.

You're white as a sheet, little Saxon . . . Why do I love you? . . . It's funny, I don't like to think of you in pain. Show me that hand. A horse bite can turn nasty. I'll put some of that juniper gin on it.

BECKET. (*Snatching his hand away*) I already have, my Lord, it's nothing.

KING. Then why do you look so pale? Show me your hand.

BECKET. (*With sudden coldness*) It's an ugly wound and you know you hate the sight of blood.

KING. (*Steps back a little, then exclaims with delight*) All this just to fetch me a drink! Wounded in the service of the King! We'll tell the others you defended me against a wild boar and I'll present you with a handsome gift this evening. What would you like?

BECKET. (*Softly*) This girl.

He adds after a pause:
I fancy her.
A pause.

KING. (*His face clouding over*) That's tiresome of you.
I fancy her too. And where that's concerned, friendship
goes by the board.
A pause. His face takes on a cunning look.
All right, then. But favor for favor. You won't forget,
will you?

BECKET. No, my prince.

KING. Favor for favor; do you give me your word as a gentleman?

BECKET. Yes, my prince.

KING. (*Draining his glass, suddenly cheerful*) Done! She's
yours. Do we take her with us or shall we have her
sent?

BECKET. I'll send two soldiers to fetch her. Listen. The
others have caught up.
*A troop of men-at-arms have come riding up be-
hind the shack during the end of the scene.*

KING. (*To the* MAN) Wash your daughter, dog, and kill
her fleas. She's going to the palace. For Milord here,
who's a Saxon too. You're pleased about that, I hope?
To BECKET *as he goes:*
Give him a gold piece. I'm feeling generous this morning.
He goes out. The MAN *looks at* BECKET *in terror.*

BECKET. No one will come and take your daughter away.
Keep her better hidden in future. And tell your son to
join the others, in the forest, he'll be safer there, now.
I think one of the soldiers saw us. Here!
He throws him a purse and goes out. When he has

gone, the MAN *snatches up the purse, then spits venomously, his face twisted with hate.*

MAN. God rot your guts! Pig!

GIRL. (*Unexpectedly*) He was handsome, that one. It is true he's taking me to the palace?

MAN. You whore! You Norman's trollop!
He hurls himself onto her and beats her savagely. The KING, BECKET *and the* BARONS *have galloped off, amid the sound of bugles. The hut and the forest backcloth disappear. We are in* BECKET's *palace.*
FOOTMEN *push on a kind of low bed-couch, with cushions and some stools. Upstage, between two pillars, a curtain behind which can be seen the shadows of banqueting guests. Singing and roars of laughter. Downstage, curled up on the bed,* GWENDOLEN *is playing a string instrument. The curtain is drawn aside.* BECKET *appears. He goes to* GWENDOLEN *while the banqueting and the laughter, punctuated by hoarse incoherent snatches of song, go on upstage.* GWENDOLEN *stops playing.*

GWENDOLEN. Are they still eating?

BECKET. Yes. They have an unimaginable capacity for absorbing food.

GWENDOLEN. (*Softly, beginning to play again*) How can my Lord spend his days and a large part of his nights with such creatures?

BECKET. (*Crouching at her feet and caressing her*) If he spent his time with learned clerics debating the sex of angels, your Lord would be even more bored, my kitten. They are as far from the true knowledge of things as mindless brutes.

GWENDOLEN. (*Gently, as she plays*) I don't always understand everything my Lord condescends to say to me . . . What I do know is that it is always very late when he comes to see me.

BECKET. (*Caressing her*) The only thing I love is coming to you. Beauty is one of the few things which don't shake one's faith in God.

GWENDOLEN. I am my Lord's war captive and I belong to him body and soul. God has willed it so, since He gave the Normans victory over my people. If the Welsh had won the war I would have married a man of my own race, at my father's castle. God did not will it so.

BECKET. (*Quietly*) That belief will do as well as any, my kitten. But, as I belong to a conquered race myself, I have a feeling that God's system is a little muddled. Go on playing.

> GWENDOLEN *starts to play again. Then she says suddenly:*

GWENDOLEN. I'm lying. You are my Lord, God or no God. And if the Welsh had been victorious, you could just as easily have stolen me from my father's castle. I should have come with you.

> *She says this gravely.* BECKET *rises abruptly and moves away. She looks up at him with anguished eyes and stops playing.*

Did I say something wrong? What is the matter with my Lord?

BECKET. Nothing. I don't like being loved. I told you that.

> *The curtain opens. The* KING *appears.*

KING. (*A little drunk*) Well, son, have you deserted us? It worked! I told you! They've tumbled to it! They're fighting with your forks! They've at last discovered that they're for poking one another's eyes out. They think it's a most ingenious little invention. You'd better go in, son, they'll break them in a minute.

> BECKET *goes behind the curtain to quieten his guests. He can be heard shouting:*

Gentlemen, gentlemen! No, no, they aren't little daggers. No, truly—they're for pronging meat . . . Look, let me show you again.

> *Huge roars of laughter behind the curtain. The* KING *has moved over to* GWENDOLEN. *He stares at her.*

KING. Was that you playing, while we were at table?

GWENDOLEN. (*With a deep curtsy*) Yes, my Lord.

KING. You have every kind of accomplishment, haven't you? Get up.

> *He lifts her to her feet, caressing her as he does so. She moves away, ill at ease. He says with a wicked smile:*

KING. Have I frightened you, my heart? We'll soon put that right.

> *He pulls the curtain aside.*

Hey there, Becket! That's enough horseplay, my fat lads! Come and hear a little music. When the belly's full, it's good to elevate the mind a bit.

> *To* GWENDOLEN:

Play!

> *The four* BARONS, *bloated with food and drink, come in with* BECKET. GWENDOLEN *has taken up her instrument again. The* KING *sprawls on the bed, behind her. The* BARONS, *with much sighing and puffing, unclasp their belts and sit down on stools, where they soon fall into a stupor.* BECKET *remains standing.*

Tell her to sing us something sad. I like sad music after dinner, it helps the digestion.

> *He hiccups.*

You always feed us far too well, Thomas. Where did you steal that cook of yours?

BECKET. I bought him, Sire. He's a Frenchman.

KING. Really? Aren't you afraid he might poison you? Tell me, how much does one pay for a French cook?

BECKET. A good one, like him, costs almost as much as a horse, my Lord.

KING. (*Genuinely outraged*) It's outrageous! What is the country coming to! No man is worth a horse! If I said "favor for favor"—remember?—and I asked you to give him to me, would you?

BECKET. Of course, my Lord.

KING. (*With a smile, gently caressing* GWENDOLEN) Well, I won't. I don't want to eat too well every day; it lowers a man's morale. Sadder, sadder, my little doe.
   He belches.
Oh, that venison! Get her to sing that lament they composed for your mother, Becket. It's my favorite song.

BECKET. I don't like anyone to sing that lament, my Lord.

KING. Why not? Are you ashamed of being a Saracen girl's son? That's half your charm, you fool! There must be some reason why you're more civilized than all the rest of us put together! I adore that song.
   GWENDOLEN *looks uncertainly at* BECKET. *There is a pause. Then the* KING *says coldly:*
That's an order, little Saxon.

BECKET. (*Inscrutably, to* GWENDOLEN) Sing.
   She strikes a few opening chords, while the KING *makes himself comfortable beside her, belching contentedly. She begins:*

GWENDOLEN. (*Singing*)

Handsome Sir Gilbert
Went to the war
One fine morning in May
To deliver the heart
Of Lord Jesus our Saviour,
From the hands of the Saracens.
Woe! Woe! Heavy is my heart
At being without love!
Woe! Woe! Heavy is my heart
All the livelong day!

KING. (*Singing*)

All the livelong day! Go on!

GWENDOLEN. As the battle raged
He swung his mighty sword
And many a Moor fell dead
But his trusty charger
Stumbled in the fray
And Sir Gilbert fell.
Woe! Woe! Heavy is my heart!
At being without love!
Woe! Woe! Heavy is my heart
All the livelong day.

Wounded in the head
Away Gilbert was led
To the Algiers market
Chained hand and foot
And sold there as a slave.

KING. (*Singing, out of tune*)
All the livelong day!

GWENDOLEN. A Saracen's daughter
Lovely as the night
Lost her heart to him
Swore to love him always
Vowed to be his wife.

Woe! Woe! Heavy is my heart

At being without love!
Woe! Woe! Heavy is my heart
All the livelong day—

KING. (*Interrupting*) It brings tears to my eyes, you know, that story. I look a brute but I'm soft as swansdown really. One can't change one's nature. I can't imagine why you don't like people to sing that song. It's wonderful to be a love child. When I look at my august parents' faces, I shudder to think what must have gone on. It's marvelous to think of your mother helping your father to escape and then coming to join him in London with you inside her. Sing us the end, girl. I adore the end.

GWENDOLEN. (*Softly*)
Then he asked the holy Father
For a priest to baptize her
And he took her as his wife
To cherish with his life
Giving her his soul
To love and keep alway.

Gay! Gay! Easy is my heart
At being full of love
Gay! Gay! Easy is my heart
To be loved alway.

KING. (*Dreamily*) Did he really love her all his life? Isn't it altered a bit in the song?

BECKET. No, my prince.

KING. (*Getting up, quite saddened*) Funny, it's the happy ending that makes me feel sad . . . Tell me, do you believe in love, Thomas?

BECKET. (*Coldly*) For my father's love for my mother, Sire, yes.
    The KING *has moved over to the* BARONS *who are*

> *now snoring on their stools. He gives them a kick
> as he passes.*

KING. They've fallen asleep, the hogs. That's their way
of showing their finer feelings. You know, my little
Saxon, sometimes I have the impression that you and
I are the only sensitive men in England. We eat with
forks and we have infinitely distinguished sentiments,
you and I. You've made a different man of me, in a
way . . . What you ought to find me now, if you
loved me, is a girl to give me a little polish. I've had
enough of whores.

> *He has come back to* GWENDOLEN. *He caresses
> her a little and then says suddenly:*

Favor for favor—do you remember?

> *A pause.*

BECKET. (*Pale*) I am your servant, my prince, and all I
have is yours. But you were also gracious enough to say
I was your friend.

KING. That's what I mean! As one friend to another it's
the thing to do!

> *A short pause. He smiles maliciously, and goes on
> caressing* GWENDOLEN *who cowers, terrified.*

You care about her then? Can you care for something?
Go on, tell me, tell me if you care about her?

> BECKET *says nothing. The* KING *smiles.*

You can't tell a lie. I know you. Not because you're
afraid of lies—I think you must be the only man I
know who isn't afraid of anything—not even Heaven—
but because it's distasteful to you. You consider it in-
elegant. What looks like morality in you is nothing
more than esthetics. Is that true or isn't it?

BECKET. (*Meeting his eyes, says softly*) It's true, my Lord.

KING. I'm not cheating if I ask for her, am I? I said "favor
for favor" and I asked you for your word of honor.

BECKET. (*Icily*) And I gave it to you.

> *A pause. They stand quite still. The* KING *looks at*

BECKET *with a wicked smile.* BECKET *does not look
at him. Then the* KING *moves briskly away.*

KING. Right. I'm off to bed. I feel like an early night
tonight. Delightful evening, Becket. You're the only
man in England who knows how to give your friends a
royal welcome.
He kicks the slumbering BARONS.
Call my guards and help me wake these porkers.
The BARONS *wake with sighs and belches as the
* KING *pushes them about, shouting:*
Come on, Barons, home! I know you're connoisseurs
of good music, but we can't listen to music all night
long. Happy evenings end in bed, eh Becket?

BECKET. (*Stiffly*) May I ask your Highness for a brief
moment's grace?

KING. Granted! Granted! I'm not a savage. I'll wait for
you both in my litter. You can say good night to me
downstairs.
He goes out, followed by the BARONS. BECKET
stands motionless for a while under GWENDOLEN's
steady gaze. Then he says quietly:

BECKET. You will have to go with him, Gwendolen.

GWENDOLEN. (*Composedly*) Did my Lord promise me
to him?

BECKET. I gave him my word as a gentleman that I
would give him anything he asked for. I never thought
it would be you.

GWENDOLEN. If he sends me away tomorrow, will my
Lord take me back?

BECKET. No.

GWENDOLEN. Shall I tell the girls to put my dresses in
the coffer?

BECKET. He'll send over for it tomorrow. Go down. One doesn't keep the King waiting. Tell him I wish him a respectful good night.

GWENDOLEN. (*Laying her viol on the bed*) I shall leave my Lord my viol. He can almost play it now.
She asks, quite naturally:
My Lord cares for nothing, in the whole world, does he?

BECKET. No.

GWENDOLEN. (*Moves to him and says gently*) You belong to a conquered race too. But through tasting too much of the honey of life, you've forgotten that even those who have been robbed of everything have one thing left to call their own.

BECKET. (*Inscrutably*) Yes, I daresay I had forgotten. There is a gap in me where honor ought to be. Go now.
GWENDOLEN *goes out.* BECKET *stands quite still. Then he goes to the bed, picks up the viol, looks at it, then throws it abruptly away. He pulls off the fur coverlet and starts to unbutton his doublet. A* GUARD *comes in, dragging the* SAXON GIRL *from the forest, whom he throws down in the middle of the room. The* KING *appears.*

KING. (*Hilariously*) Thomas, my son! You'd forgotten her! You see how careless you are! Luckily I think of everything. It seems they had to bully the father and the brother a tiny bit to get her, but anyway, here she is. You see?—I really am a friend to you, and you're wrong not to love me. You told me you fancied her. I hadn't forgotten that, you see. Sleep well, son!
He goes out, followed by the GUARD. *The* GIRL, *still dazed, looks at* BECKET *who has not moved. She recognizes him, gets to her feet and smiles at him. A long pause, then she asks with a kind of sly coquetry:*

GIRL. Shall I undress, my Lord?

BECKET. (*Who has not moved*) Of course.

> *The* GIRL *starts to undress.* BECKET *looks at her coldly, absent-mindedly whistling a few bars of his little march. Suddenly he stops, goes to the* GIRL, *who stands there dazed and half naked, and seizes her by the shoulders.*

I hope you're full of noble feelings and that all this strikes you as pretty shabby?

> *A* SERVANT *runs in wildly and halts in the doorway speechless. Before he can speak, the* KING *comes stumbling in.*

KING. (*Soberly*) I had no pleasure with her, Thomas. She let me lay her down in the litter, limp as a corpse, and then suddenly she pulled out a little knife from somewhere. There was blood everywhere . . . I feel quite sick.

> BECKET *has let go of the* GIRL. *The* KING *adds, haggard:*

She could easily have killed me instead!

> *A pause. He says abruptly:*

Send that girl away. I'm sleeping in your room tonight. I'm frightened.

> BECKET *motions to the* SERVANT, *who takes away the half-naked* GIRL. *The* KING *has thrown himself, fully dressed, onto the bed with an animal-like sigh.*

Take half the bed.

BECKET. I'll sleep on the floor, my prince.

KING. No. Lie down beside me. I don't want to be alone tonight.

> *He looks at him and murmurs:*

You loathe me, I shan't even be able to trust you now . . .

BECKET. You gave me your Seal to keep, my prince. And

the Three Lions of England which are engraved on it
keep watch over me too.

*He snuffs out the candles, all save one. It is al-
most dark.*

KING. (*His voice already thick with sleep*) I shall never
know what you're thinking . . .

BECKET *has thrown a fur coverlet over the* KING.
He lies down beside him and says quietly:

BECKET. It will be dawn soon, my prince. You must
sleep. Tomorrow we are crossing to the Continent. In
a week we will face the King of France's army and
there will be simple answers to everything at last.

He has lain down beside the KING. *A pause, during which the* KING's *snoring gradually increases.
Suddenly, the* KING *moans and tosses in his sleep.*

KING. (*Crying out*) They're after me! They're after me!
They're armed to the teeth! Stop them! Stop them!

BECKET *sits up on one elbow. He touches the* KING,
who wakes up with a great animal cry.

BECKET. My prince . . . my prince . . . sleep in peace. I'm
here.

KING. Oh . . . Thomas, it's you . . . They were after me.

*He turns over and goes back to sleep with a sigh.
Gradually he begins to snore again, softly.* BECKET
*is still on one elbow. Almost tenderly, he draws
the coverlet over the* KING.

BECKET. My prince . . . If you were my true prince, if
you were one of my race, how simple everything would
be. How tenderly I would love you, my prince, in an
ordered world. Each of us bound in fealty to the other,
head, heart and limbs, with no further questions to ask
of oneself, ever.

A pause. The KING's *snores grow louder.* BECKET
sighs and says with a little smile:

But I cheated my way, a twofold bastard, into the

ranks, and found a place among the conquerors. You can sleep peacefully though, my prince. So long as Becket is obliged to improvise his honor, he will serve you. And if one day, he meets it face to face . . .

A short pause.

But where is Becket's honor?

He lies down with a sigh, beside the KING. *The* KING's *snores grow louder still. The candle sputters. The lights grow even dimmer . . .*

THE CURTAIN FALLS

END OF ACT ONE

ACT TWO

The curtain rises on the same set of arching pillars, which now represents a forest in France. The KING's *tent, not yet open for the day, is set up among the trees. A* SENTRY *stands some way off.*

It is dawn. Crouched around a campfire, the four BARONS *are having their morning meal, in silence. After a while, one of them says:*

1ST BARON. This Becket then, who is he?
A pause. All four are fairly slow in their reactions.

2ND BARON. (*Surprised at the question*) The Chancellor of England.

1ST BARON. I know that! But who is he, exactly?

2ND BARON. The Chancellor of England, I tell you! The Chancellor of England is the Chancellor of England! I don't see what else there is to inquire into on that score.

1ST BARON. You don't understand. Look, supposing the Chancellor of England were some other man. Me, for instance . . .

2ND BARON. That's plain idiotic.

1ST BARON. I said supposing. Now, I would be Chancellor of England but I wouldn't be the same Chancellor of England as Becket is. You can follow that, can you?

2ND BARON. (*Guardedly*) Yes . . .

1ST BARON. So, I *can* ask myself the question.

2ND BARON. What question?

1ST BARON. Who is this man Becket?

2ND BARON. What do you mean, who is this man Becket? He's the Chancellor of England.

1ST BARON. Yes. But what I'm asking myself is who is he, as a man?

2ND BARON. (*Looks at him and says sorrowfully*) Have you got a pain?

1ST BARON. No, why?

2ND BARON. A Baron who asks himself questions is a sick Baron. Your sword—what's that?

1ST BARON. My sword?

2ND BARON. Yes.

1ST BARON. (*Putting his hand to the hilt*) It's my sword! And anyone who thinks different—

2ND BARON. Right. Answered like a nobleman. We peers aren't here to ask questions. We're here to give answers.

1ST BARON. Right then. Answer me.

2ND BARON. Not to questions! To orders. You aren't asked to think in the army. When you're face to face with a French man-at-arms, do you ask yourself questions?

1ST BARON. No.

2ND BARON. Does he?

1ST BARON. No.

2ND BARON. Does he?

1ST BARON. No.

2ND BARON. You just fall to and fight. If you started asking each other questions like a pair of women, you might as well bring chairs onto the battlefield. If there are any questions to be asked you can be sure they've been asked already, higher up, by cleverer heads than yours.

1ST BARON. (*Vexed*) I meant I didn't like him, that's all.

2ND BARON. Why couldn't you say so then? That we'd

have understood. You're entitled not to like him. I don't like him either, come to that. To begin with, he's a Saxon.

1ST BARON. To begin with!

3RD BARON. One thing you can't say though. You can't say he isn't a fighter. Yesterday when the King was in the thick of it, after his squire was killed, he cut his way right through the French, and he seized the King's banner and drew the enemy off and onto himself.

1ST BARON. All right! He's a good fighter!

3RD BARON. (*To* 2ND BARON) Isn't he a good fighter?

2ND BARON. (*Stubbornly*) Yes. But he's a Saxon.

1ST BARON. (*To the* 4TH BARON, *who has so far said nothing*) How about you, Regnault? What do you think of him?

4TH BARON. (*Placidly, swallowing his mouthful of food*) I'm waiting.

1ST BARON. Waiting for what?

4TH BARON. Till he shows himself. Some sorts of game are like that: you follow them all day through the forest, by sounds, or tracks, or smell. But it wouldn't do any good to charge ahead with drawn lance; you'd just spoil everything because you don't know for sure what sort of animal it is you're dealing with. You have to wait.

1ST BARON. What for?

4TH BARON. For whatever beast it is to show itself. And if you're patient it always does in the end. Animals know more than men do, nearly always, but a man has something in him that an animal hasn't got:

he knows how to wait. With this man Becket—I'll wait.

1ST BARON. For what?

4TH BARON. For him to show himself. For him to break cover.
He goes on eating.
The day he does, we'll know who he is.
BECKET's *little whistled march is heard off stage.*
BECKET *comes in, armed.*

BECKET. Good morning to you, Gentlemen.
The four BARONS *rise politely, and salute.*
Is the King still asleep?

1ST BARON. (*Stiffly*) He hasn't called yet.

BECKET. Has the camp marshal presented his list of losses?

1ST BARON. No.

BECKET. Why not?

2ND BARON. (*Surlily*) He was part of the losses.

BECKET. Oh?

1ST BARON. I was nearby when it happened. A lance knocked him off his horse. Once on the ground, the foot soldiers dealt with him.

BECKET. Poor Beaumont. He was so proud of his new armor.

2ND BARON. There must have been a chink in it then. They bled him white. On the ground. French swine!

BECKET. (*With a slight shrug*) That's war.

1ST BARON. War is a sport like any other. There are rules. In the old days, they took you for ransom. A Knight for a Knight. That was proper fighting!

BECKET. (*Smiling*) Since one has taken to sending the foot soldiery against the horses with no personal protection save a cutlass, they're a little inclined to seek out the chink in the armor of any Knight unwise enough to fall off his horse. It's repulsive, but I can understand them.

1ST BARON. If we start understanding the common soldiery war will be butchery plain and simple.

BECKET. The world is certainly tending towards butchery, Baron. The lesson of this battle, which has cost us far too much, is that we will have to form platoons of cutthroats too, that's all.

1ST BARON. And a soldier's honor, my Lord Chancellor, what of that?

BECKET. (*Dryly*) A soldier's honor, Baron, is to win victories. Let us not be hypocritical. The Norman nobility lost no time in teaching those they conquered that little point. I'll wake the King. Our entry into the city is timed for eight o'clock and the *Te Deum* in the cathedral for a quarter past nine. It would be bad policy to keep the French Bishop waiting. We want these people to collaborate with a good grace.

1ST BARON. (*Grunting*) In my day, we slaughtered the lot and marched in afterwards.

BECKET. Yes, into a dead city! I want to give the King living cities to increase his wealth. From eight o'clock this morning, I am the French people's dearest friend.

1ST BARON. What about England's honor, then?

BECKET. (*Quietly*) England's honor, Baron, in the final reckoning, has always been to succeed.

> *He goes into the* KING's *tent smiling. The four* BARONS *look at each other, hostile.*

1ST BARON. (*Muttering*) What a mentality!

4TH BARON. (*Sententiously*) We must wait for him. One day, he'll break cover.

> *The four* BARONS *move away.* BECKET *lifts the tent flap and hooks it back. The* KING *is revealed, in bed with a girl.*

KING. (*Yawning*) Good morning, son. Did you sleep well?

BECKET. A little memento from the French on my left shoulder kept me awake, Sire. I took the opportunity to do some thinking.

KING. (*Worriedly*) You think too much. You'll suffer for it, you know! It's because people think that there are problems. One day, if you go on like this, you'll think yourself into a dilemma, your big head will present you with a solution and you'll jump feet first into a hopeless mess—which you'd have done far better to ignore, like the majority of fools, who know nothing and live to a ripe old age. What do you think of my little French girl? I must say, I adore France.

BECKET. (*Smiling*) So do I, Sire, like all Englishmen.

KING. The climate's warm, the girls are pretty, the wine is good. I intend to spend at least a month here every winter.

BECKET. The only snag is, it's expensive! Nearly 2,000 casualties yesterday.

KING. Has Beaumont made out his total?

BECKET. Yes. And he added himself to the list.

KING. Wounded?

> BECKET *does not answer. The* KING *shivers. He*
> *says somberly:*

I don't like learning that people I know have died. I've
a feeling it may give Death ideas.

BECKET. My prince, shall we get down to work? We
haven't dealt with yesterday's dispatches.

KING. Yesterday we were fighting! We can't do everything.

BECKET. That was a holiday! We'll have to work twice
as hard today.

KING. Does it amuse you—working for the good of my
people? Do you mean to say you love all those folk?
To begin with they're too numerous. One can't love
them, one doesn't know them. Anyway, you're lying,
you don't love anything or anybody.

BECKET. (*Tersely*) There's one thing I do love, my
prince, and that I'm sure of. Doing what I have to do
and doing it well.

KING. (*Grinning*) Always the es—es . . . What's your
word again? I've forgotten it.

BECKET. Esthetics?

KING. Esthetics! Always the esthetic side, eh?

BECKET. Yes, my prince.

KING. (*Slapping the* GIRL's *rump*) And isn't that esthetic
too? Some people go into ecstasies over cathedrals.
But this is a work of art too! Look at that—round
as an apple . . .

> *Quite naturally, as if he were offering him a*
> *sweetmeat:*

Want her?

BECKET. (*Smiling*) Business, my Lord!

KING. (*Pouting like a schoolboy*) All right. Business. I'm
listening. Sit down.

> BECKET *sits down on the bed, beside the* KING,
> *with the* GIRL *like a fascinated rabbit in between*
> *them.*

BECKET. The news is not good, my prince.

KING. (*With a careless wave of the hand*) News never
is. That's a known fact. Life is one long web of difficulties. The secret of it—and there is one, brought to
perfection by several generations of worldly-wise phi-
losophers—is to give them no importance whatever. In
the end one difficulty swallows up the other and you
find yourself ten years later still alive with no harm
done. Things always work out.

BECKET. Yes. But badly. My prince, when you play
tennis, do you simply sit back and let things work
out? Do you wait for the ball to hit your racket and
say "It's bound to come this way eventually"?

KING. Ah, now just a minute. You're talking about things
that matter. A game of tennis is important, it amuses
me.

BECKET. And suppose I were to tell you that governing
can be as amusing as a game of tennis? Are we going
to let the others smash the ball into our court, my
prince, or shall we try to score a point, both of us,
like two good English sportsmen?

KING. (*Suddenly roused by his sporting instinct*) The
point, Begod, the point! You're right! On the court,
I sweat and strain, I fall over my feet, I half kill myself, I'll cheat if need be, but I never give up the
point!

BECKET. Well then, I'll tell you what the score is, so far.

Piecing together all the information I have received
from London since we've been on the Continent, one
thing strikes me, and that is: that there exists in England a power which has grown until it almost rivals
yours, my Lord. It is the power of your clergy.

KING. We did get them to pay the tax. That's something!

BECKET. Yes, it's a small sum of money. And they know
that Princes can always be pacified with a little money.
But those men are past masters at taking back with
one hand what they were forced to give with the other.
That's a little conjuring trick they've had centuries of
practice in.

KING. (*To the* GIRL) Pay attention, my little sparrow.
Now's your chance to educate yourself. The gentleman is saying some very profound things!

BECKET. (*In the same flippant way*) Little French sparrow, suppose you educate us instead. When you're
married—if you do marry despite the holes in your
virtue—which would you prefer, to be mistress in your
own house or to have your village priest laying down
the law there?
> *The* KING, *a little peeved, gets up on his knees
> on the bed and hides the bewildered* GIRL *under
> an eiderdown.*

KING. Talk sense, Becket! Priests are always intriguing, I
know that. But I also know that I can crush them any
time I like.

BECKET. Talk sense, Sire. If you don't do the crushing
now, in five years' time there will be two Kings in
England, the Archbishop of Canterbury and you. And
in ten years' time there will be only one.

KING. (*A bit shamefaced*) And it won't be me?

BECKET. (*Coldly*) I rather fear not.

KING. (*With a sudden shout*) Oh, yes, it will! We
   Plantagenets hold on to our own! To horse, Becket, to
   horse! For England's glory! War on the faithful! That
   will make a change for us!
>   *The eiderdown starts to toss. The* GIRL *emerges,
>   disheveled, and red in the face.*

GIRL. (*Pleadingly*) My Lord! I can't breathe!
>   *The* KING *looks at her in surprise. He had clearly
>   forgotten her. He bursts out laughing.*

KING. What are you doing there? Spying for the
   clergy? Be off. Put your clothes on and go home.
   Give her a gold piece, Thomas.
>   *The* GIRL *picks up her rags and holds them up in
>   front of her.*

GIRL. Am I to come back to the camp tonight, my Lord?

KING. (*Exasperated*) Yes. No. I don't know! We're concerned with the Archbishop now, not you! Be off.
>   *The* GIRL *disappears into the back portion of the
>   tent. The* KING *cries:*
To horse, Thomas! For England's greatness! With my
big fist and your big brain we'll do some good work,
you and I! (*With sudden concern*) Wait a second.
You can never be sure of finding another one as good
in bed.
>   *He goes to the rear of the tent and cries:*
Come back tonight, my angel! I adore you! You have
the prettiest eyes in the world!
>   *He comes downstage and says confidentially to*
>   BECKET:
You always have to tell them that, even when you pay
for it, if you want real pleasure with them. That's high
politics, too!
>   *Suddenly anxious, as his childish fear of the
>   clergy returns.*
What will God say to it all, though? After all, they're
His Bishops!

BECKET. (*With an airy gesture*) We aren't children. You know one can always come to some arrangement with God, on this earth. Make haste and dress, my prince. We're going to be late.

KING. (*Hurrying out*) I'll be ready in a second. Do I have to shave?

BECKET. (*Smiling*) It might be as well, after two days' fighting.

KING. What a fuss for a lot of conquered Frenchmen! I wonder sometimes if you aren't a bit too finicky, Thomas.
> *He goes out.* BECKET *closes the tent just as two* SOLDIERS *bring on a* YOUNG MONK, *with his hands tied.*

BECKET. What is it?

SOLDIER. We've just arrested this young monk, my Lord. He was loitering round the camp. He had a knife under his robe. We're taking him to the Provost.

BECKET. Have you got the knife?
> *The* SOLDIER *hands it to him.* BECKET *looks at it, then at the little* MONK.
What use do you have for this in your monastery?

MONK. I cut my bread with it!

BECKET. (*Amused*) Well, well. (*To the* SOLDIERS) Leave him to me. I'll question him.

SOLDIER. He's turbulent, my Lord. He struggled like a very demon. It took four of us to get his knife away and tie him up. He wounded the Sergeant. We'd have finished him there and then, only the Sergeant said there might be some information to be got out of him. That's why we're taking him to the Provost.
> *He adds:*

That's just to tell you he's a spiteful devil.

BECKET. (*Who has not taken his eyes off the little* MONK) Very well. Stand off.
> *The* SOLDIERS *move out of earshot.* BECKET *goes on looking at the boy, and playing with the knife.*

What are you doing in France? You're a Saxon.

MONK. (*Crying out despite himself*) How do you know?

BECKET. I can tell by your accent. I speak Saxon very well, as well as you speak French. Yes, you might almost pass for a Frenchman—to unpracticed ears. But I'd be careful. In your predicament, you'd do as well to be taken for a Frenchman as a Saxon. It's less unpopular.
> *A pause.*

MONK. (*Abruptly*) I'm prepared to die.

BECKET. (*Smiling*) After the deed. But before, you'll agree it's stupid.
> *He looks at the knife which he is still holding between two fingers.*

Where are you from?

MONK. (*Venomously*) Hastings!

BECKET. Hastings. And who was this kitchen implement intended for?
> *No answer.*

You couldn't hope to kill more than one man with a weapon of this sort. You didn't make the journey for the sake of an ordinary Norman soldier, I imagine.
> *The little* MONK *does not answer.*

(*Tersely*) Listen to me, my little man. They're going to put you to the torture. Have you ever seen that? I'm obliged to attend professionally from time to time. You think you'll have the necessary strength of spirit, but they're terribly ingenious and they have a knowledge of anatomy that our imbecilic doctors would do well to

emulate. One always talks. Believe me, I know. If I can
vouch that you've made a full confession, it will go
quicker for you. That's worth considering.
> *The* MONK *does not answer.*

Besides, there's an amusing detail to this affair. You are
directly under my jurisdiction. The King gave me the
deeds and livings of all the abbeys in Hastings when he
made me Chancellor.

MONK. (*Stepping back*) Are you Becket?

BECKET. Yes.
> *He looks at the knife with faint distaste.*

You didn't only use it to cut your bread. Your knife
stinks of onion, like any proper little Saxon's knife.
They're good, aren't they, the Hastings onions?
> *He looks at the knife again with a strange smile.*

You still haven't told me who it was for.
> *The* MONK *says nothing.*

If you meant it for the King, there was no sense in
that, my lad. He has three sons. Kings spring up again
like weeds! Did you imagine you could liberate your
race single-handed?

MONK. No.
> *He adds dully:*

Not my race. Myself.

BECKET. Liberate yourself from what?

MONK. My shame.

BECKET. (*With sudden gravity*) How old are you?

MONK. Sixteen.

BECKET. (*Quietly*) The Normans have occupied the is-
land for a hundred years. Shame is an old vintage. Your
father and your grandfather drank it to the dregs. The
cup is empty now.

MONK. (*Shaking his head*) No.
>   *A shadow seems to cross* BECKET's *eyes. He goes on, quietly:*

BECKET. So, one fine morning, you woke in your cell to the bell of the first offices, while it was still dark. And it was the bells that told you, a boy of sixteen, to take the whole burden of shame onto yourself?

MONK. (*With the cry of a cornered animal*) Who told you that?

BECKET. (*Softly*) I told you I was a polyglot. (*Indifferently*) I'm a Saxon too, did you know that?

MONK. (*Stonily*) Yes.

BECKET. (*Smiling*) Go on. Spit. You're dying to.
>   *The* MONK *looks at him, a little dazed, and then spits.*

BECKET. (*Smiling*) That felt good, didn't it? (*Tersely*) The King is waiting. And this conversation could go on indefinitely. But I want to keep you alive, so we can continue it one of these days.
>   *He adds lightly:*
It's pure selfishness, you know. Your life hasn't any sort of importance for me, obviously, but it's very rare for Fate to bring one face to face with one's own ghost, when young. (*Calling*) Soldier!
>   *The* SOLDIER *comes back and springs clanking to attention.*
Fetch me the Provost. Run!
>   *The* SOLDIER *runs out.* BECKET *comes back to the silent* YOUNG MONK.

Delightful day, isn't it? This early-morning sun, hot already under this light veil of mist . . . A beautiful place, France. But I'm like you, I prefer the solid mists of the Sussex downs. Sunshine is luxury. And we belong to a race which used to despise luxury, you and I.

> *The* PROVOST MARSHAL *of the camp comes in, followed by the* SOLDIER. *He is an important personage, but* BECKET *is inaccessible, even for a* PROVOST MARSHAL, *and the man's behavior shows it.*

Sir Provost, your men have arrested this monk who was loitering round the camp. He is a lay brother from the convent of Hastings and he is directly under my jurisdiction. You will make arrangements to have him sent back to England and taken to the convent, where his Abbot will keep him under supervision until my return. There is no specific charge against him, for the moment. I want him treated without brutality, but very closely watched. I hold you personally responsible for him.

PROVOST. Very good, my Lord.

> *He motions to the* SOLDIERS. *They surround the little* MONK *and take him away without a further glance from* BECKET. *Left alone,* BECKET *looks at the knife, smiles, wrinkles his nose and murmurs, with faint distaste:*

BECKET. It's touching, but it stinks, all the same.

> *He flings the knife away, and whistling his little march goes toward the tent. He goes in, calling out lightheartedly:*

Well, my prince, have you put on your Sunday best? It's time to go. We mustn't keep the Bishop waiting!

> *A sudden joyful peal of bells. The tent disappears as soon as* BECKET *has gone in. The set changes. A backcloth representing a street comes down from the flies. The permanent pillars are there, but the* SOLDIERS *lining the route have decorated them with standards. The* KING *and* BECKET *advance into the city, on horseback, preceded by two* TRUMPETERS; *the* KING *slightly ahead of* BECKET *and followed by the four* BARONS. *Acclamations from the crowd. Bells, trumpets throughout the scene.*

KING. (*Beaming as he waves*) Listen to that! They adore us, these French!

BECKET. It cost me quite a bit. I had money distributed among the populace this morning. The prosperous classes are at home, sulking, of course.

KING. Patriots?

BECKET. No. But they would have cost too much. There are also a certain number of your Highness' soldiers among the crowd, in disguise, to encourage any luke-warm elements.

KING. Why do you always make a game of destroying my illusions? I thought they loved me for myself! You're an amoral man, Becket. (*Anxiously*) Does one say amoral or immoral?

BECKET. (*Smiling*) It depends what one means.

KING. She's pretty, look—the girl on the balcony to the right there. Suppose we stopped a minute . . .

BECKET. Impossible. The Bishop is waiting in the cathedral.

KING. It would be a lot more fun than going to see a Bishop!

BECKET. My Lord, do you remember what you have to say to him?

KING. (*Waving to the crowd*) Yes, yes, yes! As if it mattered what I say to a French Bishop, whose city I've just taken by force!

BECKET. It matters a great deal. For our future policy.

KING. Am I the strongest or am I not?

BECKET. You are, today. But one must never drive one's enemy to despair. It makes him strong. Gentleness is better politics. It saps virility. A good occupational force must not crush, it must corrupt.

KING. (*Waving graciously*) What about my pleasure then? Where does that enter into your scheme of things? Suppose I charged into this heap of frog-eaters now instead of acting the goat at their *Te Deum*? I can indulge in a bit of pleasure, can't I? I'm the conqueror.

BECKET. That would be a fault. Worse, a failing. One can permit oneself anything, Sire, but one must never indulge.

KING. Yes, Papa, right, Papa. What a bore you are today. Look at that little redhead there, standing on the fountain! Give orders for the procession to follow the same route back.

> He rides on, turning his horse to watch the girl out of sight. They have gone by, the four BARONS bringing up the rear. Organ music. The standards disappear, together with the SOLDIERS. We are in the cathedral. The stage is empty.
>
> The organ is heard. Swelling chords. The organist is practicing in the empty cathedral. Then a sort of partition is pushed on, which represents the sacristy.
>
> The KING, attired for the ceremony, the BARONS, an unknown PRIEST and a CHOIRBOY come in. They seem to be waiting for something. The KING sits impatiently on a stool.

KING. Where's Becket? And what are we waiting for?

1ST BARON. He just said to wait, my Lord. It seems there's something not quite in order.

KING. (*Pacing about ill-humoredly*) What a lot of fuss for a French Bishop! What do I look like, I ask you, hanging about in this sacristy like a village bridegroom!

4TH BARON. I quite agree, my Lord! I can't think why we don't march straight in. After all, it's your cathedral now. (*Eagerly*) What do you say, my Lord? Shall we just draw our swords and charge?

KING. (*Going meekly back to his stool with a worried frown*) No. Becket wouldn't like it. And he's better than we are at knowing the right thing to do. If he told us to wait, there must be a good reason.
    BECKET *hurries in.*
Well, Becket, what's happening? We're freezing to death in here! What do the French think they're at, keeping us moldering in this sacristy?

BECKET. The order came from me, Sire. A security measure. My police are certain that a French rising was to break out during the ceremony.
    The KING *has risen. The* 2ND BARON *has drawn his sword. The other three follow suit.*

2ND BARON. God's Blood!

BECKET. Put up your swords. The King is safe in here. I have put guards on all the doors.

2ND BARON. Have we your permission to go in and deal with it, my Lord? We'll make short work of it!

3RD BARON. Just say the word, Sire! Shall we go?

BECKET. (*Curtly*) I forbid you. There aren't enough of us. I am bringing fresh troops into the city and having the cathedral evacuated. Until that is done, the King's person is in your keeping, gentlemen. But sheathe your swords. No provocation, please. We are at the mercy of a chance incident and I still have no more than the fifty escort men-at-arms in the city.

KING. (*Tugging at* BECKET's *sleeve*) Becket! Is that priest French?

BECKET. Yes. But he is part of the Bishop's immediate entourage. And the Bishop is our man.

KING. You know how reliable English Bishops are! So I leave you to guess how far we can trust a French one! That man has a funny look in his eyes.

BECKET. Who, the Bishop?

KING. No. That priest.

BECKET. (*Glances at the* PRIEST *and laughs*) Of course, my prince, he squints! I assure you that's the only disturbing thing about him! It would be tactless to ask him to leave. Besides, even if he had a dagger, you have your coat of mail and four of your Barons. I must go and supervise the evacuation of the nave.
    He starts to go. The KING *runs after him.*

KING. Becket!
     BECKET *stops.*
The choirboy?

BECKET. (*Laughing*) He's only so high!

KING. He may be a dwarf. You never know with the French.
     Drawing BECKET *aside.*
Becket, we talked a little flippantly this morning. Are you sure God isn't taking his revenge?

BECKET. (*Smiling*) Of course not. I'm afraid it's simply my police force taking fright and being a little overzealous. Policemen have a slight tendency to see assassins everywhere. They only do it to make themselves important. Bah, what does it matter? We'll hear the *Te Deum* in a deserted church, that's all.

KING. (*Bitterly*) And there was I thinking those folk adored me. Perhaps you didn't give them enough money.

BECKET. One can only buy those who are for sale, my prince. And those are just the ones who aren't dangerous. With the others, it's wolf against wolf. I'll come back straightaway and set your mind at rest.
> *He goes out. The* KING *darts anxious looks on the* PRIEST *as he paces up and down muttering his prayers.*

KING. Baron!
> *The* 4TH BARON *is nearest the* KING. *He steps forward.*

4TH BARON. (*Bellowing as usual*) My Lord?

KING. Shush! Keep an eye on that man, all four of you, and at the slightest move, leap on him.
> *There follows a little comic dumbshow by the* KING *and the* PRIEST, *who is beginning to feel uneasy too. A sudden violent knocking on the sacristy door. The* KING *starts.*
Who is it?
> *A* SOLDIER *comes in.*

SOLDIER. A messenger from London, my Lord. They sent him on here from the camp. The message is urgent.

KING. (*Worried*) I don't like it. Regnault, you go and see.
> *The* 4TH BARON *goes out and comes back again, reassured.*

4TH BARON. It's William of Corbeil, my Lord. He has urgent letters.

KING. You're sure it *is* him? It wouldn't be a Frenchman in disguise? That's an old trick.

4TH BARON. (*Roaring with laughter*) I know him, Sire!

I've drained more tankards with him than there are whiskers on his face. And the old goat has plenty!
The KING *makes a sign. The* 4TH BARON *admits the* MESSENGER, *who drops on one knee and presents his letters to the* KING.

KING. Thank you. Get up. That's a fine beard you have, William of Corbeil. Is it well stuck on?

MESSENGER. (*Rising, bewildered*) My beard, Sire?
The 4TH BARON *guffaws and slaps him on the back.*

4TH BARON. You old porcupine you!
The KING *has glanced through the letters.*

KING. Good news, gentlemen! We have one enemy less.
BECKET *comes in. The* KING *cries joyfully:*
Becket!

BECKET. Everything is going according to plan, my prince. The troops are on their way. We've only to wait here quietly, until they arrive.

KING. (*Cheerfully*) You're right, Becket, everything is going according to plan. God isn't angry with us. He has just recalled the Archbishop.

BECKET. (*In a murmur*) That little old man . . . How could that feeble body contain so much strength?

KING. Now, now, now! Don't squander your sorrow, my son. I personally consider this an excellent piece of news!

BECKET. He was the first Norman who took an interest in me. He was a true father to me. God rest his soul.

KING. He will! After all the fellow did for Him, he's gone to Heaven, don't worry. Where he'll be definitely more use to God than he was to us. So it's definitely for the best.

He pulls BECKET *to him.*

Becket! My little Becket, I think the ball's in our court now! This is the time to score a point.

He seizes his arm, tense and quite transformed.
An extraordinary idea is just creeping into my mind, Becket. A master stroke! I can't think what's got into me this morning, but I suddenly feel extremely intelligent. It probably comes of making love with a French girl last night. I am subtle, Becket, I am profound! So profound it's making my head spin. Are you sure it isn't dangerous to think too hard? Thomas, my little Thomas! Are you listening to me?

BECKET. (*Smiling at his excitement*) Yes, my prince.

KING. (*As excited as a little boy*) Are you listening carefully? Listen, Thomas! You told me once that the best ideas are the stupidest ones, but the clever thing is to think of them! Listen, Thomas! Tradition prevents me from touching the privileges of the Primacy. You follow me so far?

BECKET. Yes, my prince . . .

KING. But what if the Primate is my man? If the Archbishop of Canterbury is for the King, how can his power possibly incommodate me?

BECKET. That's an ingenious idea, my prince, but you forget that his election is a free one.

KING. No! You're forgetting the Royal Hand! Do you know what that is? When the candidate is displeasing to the Throne the King sends his Justicer to the Conclave of Bishops and it's the King who has the final say. That's an old custom too, and for once, it's in my favor! It's fully a hundred years since the Conclave of Bishops has voted contrary to the wishes of the King!

BECKET. I don't doubt it, my Lord. But we all know your Bishops. Which one of them could you rely on? Once the Primate's miter is on their heads, they grow dizzy with power.

KING. Are you asking me, Becket? I'll tell you. Someone who doesn't know what dizziness means. Someone who isn't even afraid of God. Thomas, my son, I need your help again and this time it's important. I'm sorry to deprive you of French girls and the fun of battle, my son, but pleasure will come later. You are going over to England.

BECKET. I am at your service, my prince.

KING. Can you guess what your mission will be?
    A tremor of anguish crosses BECKET's *face at what is to come.*
BECKET. No, my prince.

KING. You are going to deliver a personal letter from me to every Bishop in the land. And do you know what those letters will contain, my Thomas, my little brother? My royal wish to have you elected Primate of England.
    BECKET *has gone deathly white. He says with a forced laugh:*

BECKET. You're joking, of course, my Lord. Just look at the edifying man, the saintly man whom you would be trusting with these holy functions!
    He has opened his fine coat to display his even finer doublet.
Why, my prince, you really fooled me for a second!
    The KING *bursts out laughing.* BECKET *laughs too, rather too loudly in his relief.*
A fine Archbishop I'd have made! Look at my new shoes! They're the latest fashion in Paris. Attractive, that little upturned toe, don't you think? Quite full of unction and compunction, isn't it, Sire?

KING. (*Suddenly stops laughing*) Shut up about your shoes, Thomas! I'm in deadly earnest. I shall write those letters before noon. You will help me.
BECKET, *deathly pale, stammers:*

BECKET. But my Lord, I'm not even a priest!

KING. (*Tersely*) You're a deacon. You can take your final vows tomorrow and be ordained in a month.

BECKET. But have you considered what the Pope will say?

KING. (*Brutally*) I'll pay the price!
BECKET, *after an anguished pause, murmurs:*

BECKET. My Lord, I see now that you weren't joking. Don't do this.

KING. Why not?

BECKET. It frightens me.

KING. (*His face set and hard*) Becket, this is an order!
BECKET *stands as if turned to stone. A pause. He murmurs:*

BECKET. (*Gravely*) If I become Archbishop, I can no longer be your friend.
A burst of organ music in the cathedral. Enter an
OFFICER.

OFFICER. The church is now empty, my Lord. The Bishop and his clergy await your Highness' good pleasure.

KING. (*Roughly to* BECKET) Did you hear that, Becket? Pull yourself together. You have an odd way of taking good news. Wake up! They say we can go in now.
The procession forms with the PRIEST *and the* CHOIRBOY *leading.* BECKET *takes his place, almost reluctantly, a pace or so behind the* KING.

BECKET. (*In a murmur*) This is madness, my Lord. Don't do it. I could not serve both God and you.

KING. (*Looking straight ahead, says stonily*) You've never disappointed me, Thomas. And you are the only man I trust. You will leave tonight. Come, let's go in.
> He motions to the PRIEST. *The procession moves off and goes into the empty cathedral, as the organ swells.*
> *A moment's darkness. The organ continues to play. Then a dim light reveals* BECKET's *room. Open chests into which two* SERVANTS *are piling costly clothes.*

2ND SERVANT. (*Who is the younger of the two*) The coat with the sable trimming as well?

1ST SERVANT. Everything! You heard what he said!

2ND SERVANT. (*Grumbling*) Sables! To beggars! Who'll give them alms if they beg with that on their backs! They'll starve to death!

1ST SERVANT. (*Cackling*) They'll eat the sables! Can't you understand, you idiot! He's going to sell all this and give them the money!

2ND SERVANT. But what will he wear himself? He's got nothing left at all!
> BECKET *comes in, wearing a plain gray dressing gown.*

BECKET. Are the chests full? I want them sent over to the Jew before tonight. I want nothing left in this room but the bare walls. Gil, the fur coverlet!

1ST SERVANT. (*Regretfully*) My Lord will be cold at night.

BECKET. Do as I say.

Regretfully, the 1ST SERVANT *takes the coverlet
and puts it in the chest.*
Has the steward been told about tonight's meal? Supper
for forty in the great hall.

1ST SERVANT. He says he won't have enough gold plate,
my Lord. Are we to mix it with the silver dishes?

BECKET. Tell him to lay the table with the wooden platters and earthenware bowls from the kitchens. The
plate has been sold. The Jew will send over for it late
this afternoon.

1ST SERVANT. (*Dazed*) The earthenware bowls and the
wooden platters. Yes, my Lord. And the steward says
could he have your list of invitations fairly soon, my
Lord. He only has three runners and he's afraid there
won't be time to—

BECKET. There are no invitations. The great doors will
be thrown open and you will go out into the street and
tell the poor they are dining with me tonight.

1ST SERVANT. (*Appalled*) Very good, my Lord.
He is about to go. BECKET *calls him back.*

BECKET. I want the service to be impeccable. The dishes
presented to each guest first, with full ceremony, just as
for princes. Go now.
The two SERVANTS *go out.* BECKET, *left alone,
casually looks over one or two articles of clothing
in the chests. He murmurs:*
I must say it was all very pretty stuff.
He drops the lid and bursts out laughing.
A prick of vanity! The mark of an upstart. A truly saintly man would never have done the whole thing in one
day. Nobody will ever believe it's genuine.
*He turns to the jeweled crucifix above the bed and
says simply:*
I hope You haven't inspired me with all these holy reso-
lutions in order to make me look ridiculous, Lord. It's

all so new to me. I'm setting about it a little clumsily
perhaps.

*He looks at the crucifix and with a swift gesture
takes it off the wall.*

And you're far too sumptuous too. Precious stones
around your bleeding Body . . . I shall give you to
some poor village church.

*He lays the crucifix on the chest. He looks around
the room, happy, lighthearted, and murmurs:*

It's like leaving for a holiday. Forgive me, Lord, but I
never enjoyed myself so much in my whole life. I
don't believe You are a sad God. The joy I feel in shed-
ding all my riches must be part of Your divine intentions.

*He goes behind the curtain into the antechamber
where he can be heard gaily whistling an old English marching song. He comes back a second later,
his bare feet in sandals, and wearing a monk's
coarse woolen robe. He draws the curtain across
again and murmurs:*

BECKET. There. Farewell, Becket. I wish there had been
something I had regretted parting with, so I could offer it to You.

He goes to the crucifix and says simply:

Lord, are You sure You are not tempting me? It all
seems far too easy.

He drops to his knees and prays.

CURTAIN

END OF ACT TWO

ACT THREE

A room in the KING's *palace. The two* QUEENS, *the* QUEEN MOTHER *and the* YOUNG QUEEN, *are on stage, working at their tapestry. The* KING's *two* SONS, *one considerably older than the other, are playing in a corner, on the floor. The* KING *is in another corner, playing at cup-and-ball. After several unsuccessful attempts to catch the ball in the cup, he throws down the toy and exclaims irritably:*

KING. Forty beggars! He invited forty beggars to dinner!

QUEEN MOTHER. The dramatic gesture, as usual! I always said you had misplaced your confidence, my son.

KING. (*Pacing up and down*) Madam, I am very particular where I place my confidence. I only ever did it once in my whole life and I am still convinced I was right. But there's a great deal we don't understand! Thomas is ten times more intelligent than all of us put together.

QUEEN MOTHER. (*Reprovingly*) You are talking about royalty, my son.

KING. (*Grunting*) What of it? Intelligence has been shared out on a different basis.

YOUNG QUEEN. It seems he has sold his gold plate and all his rich clothes to a Jew. He wears an ordinary homespun habit now.

QUEEN MOTHER. I see that as a sign of ostentation, if nothing worse! One can become a saintly man, certainly, but not in a single day. I've never liked the man. You were insane to make him so powerful.

KING. (*Crying out*) He is my friend!

QUEEN MOTHER. (*Acidly*) More's the pity.

YOUNG QUEEN. He is your friend in debauchery. It was he who lured you away from your duty towards me. It was he who first took you to the whorehouses!

KING. (*Furious*) Rubbish, Madam! I didn't need anybody to lure me away from my duty towards you. I made you three children, very conscientiously. Phew! My duty is done for a while.

YOUNG QUEEN. (*Stung*) When that libertine loses the evil influence he has on you, you will come to appreciate

the joys of family life again. Pray Heaven he disobeys
you!

KING. The joys of family life are limited, Madam. To be
perfectly frank, you bore me. You and your eternal
backbiting, over your everlasting tapestry, the pair
of you! That's no sustenance for a man!
>   *He trots about the room, furious, and comes to a*
>   *halt behind their chairs.*
If at least it had some artistic merit. My ancestress Ma-
thilda, while she was waiting for her husband to finish
carving out his kingdom, now *she* embroidered a
masterpiece—which they left behind in Bayeux, more's
the pity. But that! It's beyond belief it's so mediocre.

YOUNG QUEEN. (*Nettled*) We can only use the gifts we're
born with.

KING. Yes. And yours are meager.
>   *He glances out of the window once more to look*
>   *at the time, and says with a sigh:*
I've been bored to tears for a whole month. Not a soul
to talk to. After his nomination, not wanting to seem
in too indecent a hurry, I leave him alone to carry out
his pastoral tour. Now, back he comes at last, I summon him to the palace and he's late.
>   *He looks out of the window again and exclaims:*
Ah! Someone at the sentry post!
>   *He turns away, disappointed.*
No, it's only a monk.
>   *He wanders about the room, aimlessly. He goes*
>   *over to join the children, and watches them play-*
>   *ing for a while.*
(*Sourly*) Charming babes. Men in the making. Sly and
obtuse already. And to think one is expected to be
dewy-eyed over creatures like that, merely because
they aren't yet big enough to be hated or despised.
Which is the elder of you two?

ELDER BOY. (*Rising*) I am, Sir.

KING. What's your name again?

ELDER BOY. Henry III.

KING. (*Sharply*) Not yet, Sir! Number II is in the best of health. (*To the* QUEEN) You've brought them up well! Do you think of yourself as Regent already? And you wonder that I shun your bedchamber? I don't care to make love with my widow.
> *An* OFFICER *comes in.*

OFFICER. A messenger from the Archbishop, my Lord.

KING. (*Beside himself with rage*) A messenger! A messenger! I summoned the Archbishop Primate in person!
> *He turns to the women, suddenly uneasy, almost touching.*
Perhaps he's ill? That would explain everything.

QUEEN MOTHER. (*Bitterly*) That's too much to hope for.

KING. (*Raging*) You'd like to see him dead, wouldn't you, you females—because he loves me? If he hasn't come, it's because he's dying! Send the man in, quickly! O my Thomas . . .
> *The* OFFICER *goes and admits the* MONK. *The* KING *hurries over to him.*
Who are you? Is Becket ill?

MONK. (*Falling on one knee*) My Lord, I am William son of Etienne, secretary to his Grace the Archbishop.

KING. Is your master seriously ill?

MONK. No, my Lord. His Grace is in good health. He has charged me to deliver this letter with his deepest respects—and to give your Highness this.
> *He bows lower and hands something to the* KING.

KING. (*Stunned*) The Seal? Why has he sent me back the Seal?

*He unrolls the parchment and reads it in silence.
His face hardens. He says curtly, without looking
at the* MONK:

You have carried out your mission. Go.
The MONK *rises and turns to go.*

MONK. Is there an answer from your Highness for his
Grace the Archbishop?

KING. (*Harshly*) No!
The MONK *goes out. The* KING *stands still a moment, at a loss, then flings himself onto his
throne, glowering. The women exchange a con-
spiratorial look. The* QUEEN MOTHER *rises and
goes to him.*

QUEEN MOTHER. (*Insidiously*) Well, my son, what does
your friend say in his letter?

KING. (*Bawling*) Get out! Get out, both of you! And
take your royal vermin with you! I am alone!
Frightened, the QUEENS *hurry out with the children. The* KING *stands there a moment, reeling a
little, as if stunned by the blow. Then he collapses
onto the throne and sobs like a child.*

(*Moaning*) O my Thomas!
*He remains a moment prostrate, then collects
himself and sits up. He looks at the Seal in his
hand and says between clenched teeth:*

You've sent me back the Three Lions of England, like a
little boy who doesn't want to play with me any more.
You think you have God's honor to defend now! I
would have gone to war with all England's might behind
me, and against England's interests, to defend you, little Saxon. I would have given the honor of the Kingdom laughingly . . . for you . . . Only I loved you and
you didn't love me . . . that's the difference.
*His face hardens. He adds between clenched
teeth:*

Thanks all the same for this last gift as you desert me.
I shall learn to be alone.
He goes out. The lights dim. SERVANTS *remove the*

*furniture. When the lights go up again, the perma-
nent set, with the pillars, is empty.
A bare church; a man half hidden under a dark
cloak is waiting behind a pillar. It is the* KING.
Closing chords of organ music. Enter GILBERT
FOLLIOT, *Bishop of London, followed by his*
CLERGY. *He has just said Mass. The* KING *goes to
him.*

Bishop . . .

FOLLIOT. (*Stepping back*) What do you want, fellow?
*His acolytes are about to step between them,
when he exclaims:*
The King!

KING. Yes.

FOLLIOT. Alone, without an escort, and dressed like a
common squire?

KING. The King nevertheless. Bishop, I would like to
make a confession.

FOLLIOT. (*With a touch of suspicion*) I am the Bishop of
London. The King has his own Confessor. That is an
important Court appointment and it has its preroga-
tives.

KING. The choice of priest for Holy Confession is open,
Bishop, even for a King.
FOLLIOT *motions to his* CLERGY, *who draw away.*
Anyway, my confession will be short, and I'm not ask-
ing for absolution. I have something much worse than
a sin on my conscience, Bishop: a mistake. A foolish
mistake.
FOLLIOT *says nothing.*
I ordered you to vote for Thomas Becket at the Council
of Clarendon. I repent of it.

FOLLIOT. (*Inscrutably*) We bowed before the Royal
Hand.

KING. Reluctantly, I know. It took me thirteen weeks of authority and patience to crush the small uncrushable opposition of which you were the head, Bishop. On the day the Council met you looked green. They told me you fell seriously ill afterwards.

FOLLIOT. (*Impenetrably*) God cured me.

KING. Very good of Him. But He is rather inclined to look after His own, to the exclusion of anyone else. He let me fall ill without lifting a finger! And I must cure myself without divine intervention. I have the Archbishop on my stomach. A big hard lump I shall have to vomit back. What does the Norman clergy think of him?

FOLLIOT. (*Reserved*) His Grace seems to have the reins of the Church of England well in hand. Those who are in close contact with him even say that he behaves like a holy man.

KING. (*With grudging admiration*) It's a bit sudden, but nothing he does ever surprises me. God knows what the brute is capable of, for good or for evil. Bishop, let us be frank with each other. Is the Church very interested in holy men?

FOLLIOT. (*With the ghost of a smile*) The Church has been wise for so long, your Highness, that she could not have failed to realize that the temptation of saintliness is one of the most insidious and fearsome snares the devil can lay for her priests. The administration of the realm of souls, with the temporal difficulties it carries with it, chiefly demands, as in all administrations, competent administrators. The Roman Catholic Church has its Saints, it invokes their benevolent intercession, it prays to them. But it has no need to create others. That is superfluous. And dangerous.

KING. You seem to be a man one can talk to, Bishop. I misjudged you. Friendship blinded me.

FOLLIOT. (*Still impenetrable*) Friendship is a fine thing.

KING. (*Suddenly hoarse*) It's a domestic animal, a living, tender thing. It seems to be all eyes, forever gazing at you, warming you. You don't see its teeth. But it's a beast with one curious characteristic. It is only after death that it bites.

FOLLIOT. (*Prudently*) Is the King's friendship for Thomas Becket dead, your Highness?

KING. Yes, Bishop. It died quite suddenly. A sort of heart failure.

FOLLIOT. A curious phenomenon, your Highness, but quite frequent.

KING. (*Taking his arm suddenly*) I hate Becket now, Bishop. There is nothing more in common between that man and me than this creature tearing at my guts. I can't bear it any more. I shall have to turn it loose on him. But I am the King; what they conventionally call my greatness stands in my way. I need somebody.

FOLLIOT. (*Stiffening*) I do not wish to serve anything but the Church.

KING. Let us talk like grown men, Bishop. We went in hand in hand to conquer, pillage and ransom England. We quarrel, we try to cheat each other of a penny or two, but Heaven and Earth still have one or two common interests. Do you know what I have just obtained from the Pope? His Blessing to go and murder Catholic Ireland, in the name of the Faith. Yes, a sort of crusade to impose Norman barons and clergy on the Irish, with our swords and standards solemnly blessed as if we were off to give the Turks a drubbing. The only condition: a little piece of silver per household per year, for St. Peter's pence, which the native clergy of Ireland is loath to part with and which I have undertaken to make them pay. It's a mere pittance. But at

the end of the year it will add up to a pretty sum.
Rome knows how to do her accounts.

FOLLIOT. (*Terror-stricken*) There are some things one
should never say, your Highness: one should even try
not to know about them, so long as one is not directly concerned with them.

KING. (*Smiling*) We are alone, Bishop, and the church
is empty.

FOLLIOT. The church is never empty. A little red lamp
burns in front of the High Altar.

KING. (*Impatiently*) Bishop, I like playing games, but
only with boys of my own age! Do you take me for
one of your sheep, holy pastor? The One whom that
little red lamp honors read into your innermost heart
and mine a long time ago. Of your cupidity and my
hatred, He knows all there is to know.
    FOLLIOT *withdraws into his shell. The* KING *cries
    irritably:*
If that's the way you feel you must become a monk,
Bishop! Wear a hair shirt on your naked back and go
and hide yourself in a monastery to pray! The
Bishopric of London, for the purehearted son of a
Thames waterman, is too much, or too little!
    A pause.

FOLLIOT. (*Impassively*) If, as is my duty, I disregard
my private feelings, I must admit that his Grace the
Archbishop has so far done nothing which has not been
in the interests of Mother Church.

KING. (*Eying him, says jovially*) I can see your game,
my little friend. You mean to cost me a lot of money.
But I'm rich—thanks to Becket, who has succeeded in
making you pay the Absentee Tax. And it seems to me
eminently ethical that a part of the Church's gold
should find its way, via you, back to the Church. Besides, if we want to keep this on a moral basis, Holy

Bishop, you can tell yourself that as the greatness of
the Church and that of the State are closely linked,
in serving me, you will in the long run be working for
the consolidation of the Catholic Faith.

FOLLIOT. (*Contemplating him with curiosity*) I had always taken your Highness for a great adolescent lout
who cared only for his pleasure.

KING. One can be wrong about people, Bishop. I made
the same mistake. (*With a sudden cry*) O my
Thomas . . .

FOLLIOT. (*Fiercely*) You love him, your Highness! You
still love him! You love that mitered hog, that im-
postor, that Saxon bastard, that little guttersnipe!

KING. (*Seizing him by the throat*) Yes, I love him! But
that's my affair, priest! All I confided to you was my
hatred. I'll pay you to rid me of him, but don't ever
speak ill of him to me. Or we'll fight it out as man
to man!

FOLLIOT. Highness, you're choking me!

KING. (*Abruptly releasing him*) We will meet again tomorrow, my Lord Bishop, and we'll go over the details
of our enterprise together. You will be officially summoned to the palace on some pretext or other—my
good works in your London Diocese, say—where I
am your chief parishioner. But it won't be the poor
and needy we'll discuss. My poor can wait. The Kingdom they pin their hopes on is eternal.

> The KING *goes out.* GILBERT FOLLIOT *remains mo-
> tionless. His* CLERGY *join him timidly. He takes
> his crook and goes out with dignity, but not be-
> fore one of his Canons has discreetly adjusted his
> miter, which was knocked askew in the recent
> struggle.*
> *They have gone out.*

The lighting changes. Curtains between the pillars. The episcopal palace.
Morning. A PRIEST *enters, leading two* MONKS *and the* YOUNG MONK *from the convent of Hastings.*

PRIEST. His Grace will receive you here.
The two MONKS *are impressed. They push the* YOUNG MONK *about a little.*

1ST MONK. Stand up straight. Kiss his Grace's ring and try to answer his questions with humility, or I'll tan your backside for you!

2ND MONK. I suppose you thought he'd forgotten all about you? The great never forget anything. And don't you act proud with him or you'll be sorry.
Enter BECKET, *wearing a coarse monk's robe.*

BECKET. Well, brothers, is it fine over in Hastings?
He gives them his ring to kiss.

1ST MONK. Foggy, my Lord.

BECKET. (*Smiling*) Then it's fine in Hastings. We always think fondly of our Abbey there and we intend to visit it soon, when our new duties grant us a moment's respite. How has this young man been behaving? Has he given our Abbot much trouble?

2ND MONK. A proper mule, my Lord. Father Abbot tried kindness, as you recommended, but he soon had to have recourse to the dungeon and bread and water, and even to the whip. Nothing has any effect. The stubborn little wretch is just the same; all defiance and insults. He has fallen into the sin of pride. Nothing I know of will pull him out of that!

1ST MONK. Save a good kick in the rump perhaps—if your Grace will pardon the expression. (*To the boy*) Stand up straight.

BECKET. (*To the boy*) Pay attention to your brother.

Stand up straight. As a rule the sin of pride stiffens a man's back. Look me in the face.
The YOUNG MONK *looks at him.*
Good.
     BECKET *looks at the boy for a while, then turns to the* MONKS.
You will be taken to the kitchens where you can refresh yourselves before you leave, brothers. They have orders to treat you well. Don't spurn our hospitality; we relieve you, for today, of your vows of abstinence, and we fondly hope you will do honor to our bill of fare. Greet your father Abbot in Jesus on our behalf.

2ND MONK. (*Hesitantly*) And the lad?

BECKET. We will keep him here.

1ST MONK. Watch out for him, your Grace. He's vicious.

BECKET. (*Smiling*) We are not afraid.
     The MONKS *go out.* BECKET *and the* YOUNG MONK *remain, facing each other.*
Why do you hold yourself so badly?

YOUNG MONK. I don't want to look people in the face any more.

BECKET. I'll teach you. That will be your first lesson. Look at me.
     The boy gives him a sidelong glance.
Better than that.
     The boy looks at him.
Are you still bearing the full weight of England's shame alone? Is it that shame which bends your back like that?

YOUNG MONK. Yes.

BECKET. If I took over half of it, would it weigh less heavy?

He motions to the PRIEST.

Show in their Lordships the Bishops. You'll soon see that being alone is not a privilege reserved entirely for you.

The BISHOPS *come in.* BECKET *leads the* YOUNG MONK *into a corner.*

You stay here in the corner and hold my tablets. I ask only one thing. Don't leap at their throats; you'd complicate everything.

He motions to the BISHOPS *who remain standing.*

FOLLIOT. Your Grace, I am afraid this meeting may be a pointless one. You insisted—against our advice—on attacking the King openly. Even before the three excommunications which you asked us to sanction could be made public, the King has hit back. His Grand Justicer Richard de Lacy has just arrived in your antechamber and is demanding to see you in the name of the King. He is the bearer of an official order summoning you to appear before his assembled Council within twenty-four hours and there to answer the charges made against you.

BECKET. Of what is the King accusing me?

FOLLIOT. Prevarication. Following the examination of accounts by his Privy Council, his Highness demands a considerable sum still outstanding on your administration of the Treasury.

BECKET. When I resigned the Chancellorship I handed over my ledgers to the Grand Justicer who acquitted me of all subsequent dues and claims. What does the King demand?

OXFORD. Forty thousand marks in fine gold.

BECKET. (*Smiling*) I don't believe there was ever as much money in all the coffers of all England in all the time I was Chancellor. But a clever clerk can soon change that . . . The King has closed his fist and I am like a fly inside it.

He smiles and looks at him.

I have the impression, gentlemen, that you must be feeling something very akin to relief.

YORK. We advised you against open opposition.

BECKET. William of Aynsford, incited by the King, struck down the priest I had appointed to the Parish of his Lordship's See, on the pretext that his Highness disapproved of my choice. Am I to look on while my priests are murdered?

FOLLIOT. It is not for you to appoint a priest to a free fief! There is not a Norman, layman or cleric, who will ever concede that. It would mean reviewing the entire legal system of the Conquest. Everything can be called into question in England except the fact that it was conquered in 1066. England is the land of law and of the most scrupulous respect for the law; but the law begins at that date only, or England as such ceases to exist.

BECKET. Bishop, must I remind you that we are men of God and that we have an Honor to defend, which dates from all eternity?

OXFORD. (*Quietly*) This excommunication was bad policy, your Grace. William of Aynsford is a companion of the King.

BECKET. (*Smiling*) I know him very well. He's a charming man. I have drained many a tankard with him.

YORK. (*Yelping*) And his wife is my second cousin!

BECKET. That is a detail I deplore, my Lord Bishop, but he has killed one of my priests. If I do not defend my priests, who will? Gilbert of Clare has indicted before his court of justice a churchman who was under our exclusive jurisdiction.

YORK. An interesting victim I must say! He deserved the rope a hundred times over. The man was accused of rape and murder. Wouldn't it have been cleverer to let the wretch hang—and have peace?

BECKET. "I bring not peace but the sword." Your Lordship must I'm sure have read that somewhere. I am not interested in what this man is guilty of. If I allow my priests to be tried by a secular tribunal; if I let Robert de Vere abduct our tonsured clerics from our monasteries, as he has just done, on the grounds that the man was one of his serfs who had escaped land bondage, I don't give much for our freedom and our chances of survival in five years' time, my Lord. I have excommunicated Gilbert of Clare, Robert de Vere and William of Aynsford. The Kingdom of God must be defended like any other Kingdom. Do you think that Right has only to show it's handsome face for everything to drop in its lap? Without Might, its old enemy, Right counts for nothing.

YORK. What Might? Let us not indulge in empty words. The King is Might and he is the law.

BECKET. He is the written law, but there is another, unwritten law, which always makes Kings bend the neck eventually.
    He looks at them for a moment and smiles.
I was a profligate, gentlemen, perhaps a libertine, in any case, a worldly man. I loved living and I laughed at all these things. But you passed the burden on to me and now I have to carry it. I have rolled up my sleeves and taken it on my back and nothing will ever make me set it down again. I thank your Lordships. The council is adjourned and I have made my decision. I shall stand by these three excommunications. I shall appear tomorrow before the King's supreme court of Justice.

The BISHOPS *look at one another in surprise, then bow and go out.* BECKET *turns to the* YOUNG MONK:

Well, does the shame weigh less heavy now?

YOUNG MONK. Yes.

BECKET. (*Leading him off and laughing*) Then stand up straight!

> *The drapes close. Distant trumpets. The* KING *comes out from behind the curtains and turns to peep through them at something. A pause. Then* GILBERT FOLLIOT *comes hurrying in.*

KING. What's happening? I can't see a thing from up here.

FOLLIOT. Legal procedure is taking its course, your Highness. The third summons has been delivered. He has not appeared. In a moment he will be condemned in absentia. Once prevarication is established, our Dean the Bishop of Chichester will go to see him and communicate according to the terms of the ancient Charter of the Church of England, our corporated repudiation of allegiance, absolving us of obedience to him—and our intention to report him to our Holy Father the Pope. I shall then, as Bishop of London, step forward and publicly accuse Becket of having celebrated, in contempt of the King, a sacrilegious Mass at the instigation of the Evil Spirit.

KING. (*Anxiously*) Isn't that going rather far?

FOLLIOT. Of course. It won't fool anyone, but it always works. The assembly will then go out to vote, in order of precedence, and return a verdict of imprisonment. The sentence is already drawn up.

KING. Unanimously?

FOLLIOT. We are all Normans. The rest is your Highness' concern. It will merely be a matter of carrying out the sentence.

KING. (*Staggering suddenly*) O my Thomas!

FOLLIOT. (*Impassively*) I can still stop the machine, your Highness.

KING. (*Hesitates a second then says*) No. Go.
    FOLLIOT *goes out. The* KING *goes back to his place, behind the curtain.*
    The two QUEENS *come into the room, and join the* KING. *All three stand and peer through the curtain. A pause.*

YOUNG QUEEN. He's doomed, isn't he?

KING. (*Dully*) Yes.

YOUNG QUEEN. At last!
    The KING *turns on her, his face twisted with hate.*

KING. I forbid you to gloat!

YOUNG QUEEN. At seeing your enemy perish—why not?

KING. (*Frothing*) Becket is my enemy, but in the human balance, bastard as he is, and naked as his mother made him, he weighs a hundred times more than you do, Madam, with your crown and all your jewels and your august father the Emperor into the bargain. Becket is attacking me and he has betrayed me. I am forced to fight him and crush him, but at least he gave me, with open hands, everything that is at all good in me. And you have never given me anything but your carping mediocrity, your everlasting obsession with your puny little person and what you thought was due to it. That is why I forbid you to smile as he lies dying!

YOUNG QUEEN. I gave you my youth! I gave you your children!

KING. (*Shouting*) I don't like my children! And as for your youth—that dusty flower pressed in a hymnbook since you were twelve years old, with its watery blood and its insipid scent—you can say farewell to that without a tear. With age, bigotry and malice may perhaps give some spice to your character. Your body was an empty desert, Madam!—which duty forced me to wander in alone. But you have never been a wife to me! And Becket was my friend, red-blooded, generous and full of strength!

He is shaken by a sob.

O my Thomas!

The QUEEN MOTHER *moves over to him.*

QUEEN MOTHER. (*Haughtily*) And I, my son, I gave you nothing either, I suppose?

KING. (*Recovers his composure, glares at her and says dully*) Life. Yes. Thank you. But after that I never saw you save in a passage, dressed for a Ball, or in your crown and ermine mantle, ten minutes before official ceremonies, where you were forced to tolerate my presence. I have always been alone, and no one on this earth has ever loved me except Becket!

QUEEN MOTHER. (*Bitterly*) Well, call him back! Absolve him, since he loves you! Give him supreme power then! But do something!

KING. I am. I'm learning to be alone again, Madam. As usual.

A PAGE *comes in, breathless.*

Well? What's happening? How far have they got?

PAGE. My Liege, Thomas Becket appeared just when everyone had given him up; sick, deathly pale, in full pontifical regalia and carrying his own heavy silver cross. He walked the whole length of the hall without anyone daring to stop him, and when Robert Duke of Leicester, who was to read out his sentence, began the consecrated words, he stopped with a gesture and forbade him, in God's name, to pronounce judgment against him, his spiritual Father. Then he walked back through the crowd, which parted for him in silence. He has just left.

KING. (*Unable to hide his delight*) Well played, Thomas! One point to you.

> *He checks himself, embarrassed, and then says:*

And what about my Barons?

PAGE. Their hands flew to their swords with cries of "Traitor! Perjurer! Arrest him! Miserable wretch! Hear your sentence!" But not one of them dared move, or touch the sacred ornaments.

KING. (*With a roar*) The fools! I am surrounded by fools and the only intelligent man in my Kingdom is against me!

PAGE. (*Continuing his story*) Then, on the threshold, he turned, looked at them coldly as they shouted in their impotence, and he said that not so long ago he could have answered their challenge sword in hand. Now he could no longer do it, but he begged them to remember that there was a time when he met strength with strength.

KING. (*Jubilantly*) He could beat them all! All, I tell you! On horseback, on foot, with a mace, with a lance, with a sword! In the lists they fell to him like ninepins!

PAGE. And his eyes were so cold, and so ironic—even though all he had in his hand was his episcopal crook— that one by one, they fell silent. Only then did he turn and go out. They say he has given orders to invite all the beggars of the city to sup at his house tonight.

KING. (*Somberly*) And what about the Bishop of London, who was going to reduce him to powder? What about my busy friend Gilbert Folliot?

PAGE. He had a horrible fit of rage trying to incite the
crowd, he let out a screech of foul abuse and then he
fainted. They are bringing him round now.

> The KING *suddenly bursts into a shout of irrepres-
> sible laughter, and, watched by the two outraged
> QUEENS, collapses into the PAGE's arms, breathless
> and helpless with mirth.*

KING. It's too funny! It's too funny!

QUEEN MOTHER. (*Coldly*) You will laugh less heartily tomorrow, my son. If you don't stop him, Becket will
reach the coast tonight, ask asylum of the King of
France and jeer at you, unpunished, from across the
Channel.

> *She sweeps out with the* YOUNG QUEEN. *Suddenly,
> the* KING *stops laughing and runs out.*
> *The light changes. Curtains part. We are at the
> Court of* LOUIS, KING OF FRANCE. *He is sitting in
> the middle of the courtroom, very erect on his
> throne. He is a burly man with intelligent eyes.*

LOUIS. (*To his* BARONS) Gentlemen, we are in France and
a fart on England's King—as the song goes.

1ST BARON. Your Majesty cannot *not* receive his Ambassadors Extraordinary!

LOUIS. Ordinary, or extraordinary, I am at home to all
ambassadors. It's my job. I shall receive them.

1ST BARON. They have been waiting in your Majesty's
anteroom for over an hour, Sire.

LOUIS. Let them wait. That's *their* job. An ambassador is
made for pacing about an antechamber. I know what
they are going to ask me.

2ND BARON. The extradition of a felon is a courtesy due
from one crowned head to another.

LOUIS. My dear man, crowned heads can play the little
game of courtesy but nations owe each other none. My
right to play the courteous gentleman stops where
France's interests begin. And France's interests consist
in making things as difficult as possible for England—a
thing England never hesitates to do to us. The Archbishop is a millstone round Henry Plantagenet's neck.
Long live the Archbishop! Anyway, I like the fellow.

2ND BARON. My gracious sovereign is master. And so long
as our foreign policy permits us to expect nothing of
King Henry—

LOUIS. For the time being, it is an excellent thing to stiff-
en our attitude. Remember the Montmirail affair. We
only signed the peace treaty with Henry on condition
that he granted to spare the lives of the refugees from
Brittany and Poitou whom he asked us to hand over to
him. Two months later all of them had lost their heads.
That directly touched my personal honor. I was not
strong enough at the time, so I had to pretend I hadn't
heard of these men's execution. And I continued to
lavish smiles on my English cousin. But praise God our
affairs have taken a turn for the better. And today *he*
needs *us*. So I will now proceed to remember my honor.
Show in the ambassadors.

    Exit 1ST BARON. *He comes back with* FOLLIOT *and
the* DUKE OF ARUNDEL.

1ST BARON. Permit me to introduce to your Majesty the
two envoys extraordinary from his Highness Henry
of England; his Grace the Bishop of London and the
Duke of Arundel.

LOUIS. (*With a friendly wave to the* DUKE) Greetings to
you, Milord. I have not forgotten your amazing ex-
ploits at the last tournament at Calais. Do you still
wield a lance as mightily as you did, Milord?

ARUNDEL. (*With a gratified bow*) I hope so, Sire.

LOUIS. We hope that our friendly relations with your gracious master will allow us to appreciate your jousting skill again before long, on the occasion of the forthcoming festivities.

    FOLLIOT *has unrolled a parchment.*

Bishop, I see you have a letter for us from your master. We are listening.

FOLLIOT. (*Bows again and starts to read*) "To my Lord and friend Louis, King of the French; Henry, King of England, Duke of Normandy, Duke of Aquitaine and Count of Anjou: Learn that Thomas, former Archbishop of Canterbury, after a public trial held at my court by the plenary assembly of the Barons of my realm has been found guilty of fraud, perjury and treason towards me. He has forthwith fled my Kingdom as a traitor, and with evil intent. I therefore entreat you not to allow this criminal, nor any of his adherents, to reside upon your territories, nor to permit any of your vassals to give help, support or counsel to this my greatest enemy. For I solemnly declare that your enemies or those of your Realm would receive none from me or my subjects. I expect you to assist me in the vindication of my honor and the punishment of my enemy, as you would wish me to do for you, should the need arise."

    A pause. FOLLIOT *bows very low and hands the parchment to the* KING *who rolls it up casually and hands it to one of the* BARONS.

LOUIS. Gentlemen, we have listened attentively to our gracious cousin's request and we take good note of it. Our chancellery will draft a reply which will be sent to you tomorrow. All we can do at the moment, is express our surprise. No news had reached us of the presence of the Archbishop of Canterbury on our domains.

FOLLIOT. (*Tersely*) Sire, the former Archbishop has taken refuge at the Abbey of St. Martin, near Saint-Omer.

LOUIS. (*Still gracious*) My Lord Bishop, we flatter ourselves that there is some order in our Kingdom. If he
were there, we would certainly have been informed.

> *He makes a gesture of dismissal. The Ambassadors
> bow low and go out backwards, ushered out by
> the* 1ST BARON. *Immediately,* LOUIS *says to the*
> 2ND BARON:

Show in Thomas Becket and leave us.

> *The* 2ND BARON *goes out and a second later admits*
> THOMAS, *dressed in a monk's robe.* THOMAS *drops
> onto one knee. The* BARON *goes out.*

(*Kindly*) Rise, Thomas Becket. And greet us as the
Primate of England. The bow is enough—and if I know
my etiquette, you are entitled to a slight nod of the
head from me. There, that's done. I would even be required to kiss your ring, if your visit were an official one.
But I have the impression that it isn't, am I right?

BECKET. (*With a smile*) No, Sire. I am only an exile.

LOUIS. (*Graciously*) That too is an important title, in
France.

BECKET. I am afraid it is the only one I have left. My
property has been seized and distributed to those who
served the King against me; letters have been sent
to the Duke of Flanders and all his Barons enjoining
them to seize my person. John, Bishop of Poitiers, who
was suspected of wanting to grant me asylum, has just
been poisoned.

LOUIS. (*Smiling*) In fact you are a very dangerous man.

BECKET. I'm afraid so.

LOUIS. (*Unperturbed*) We like danger, Becket. And if the
King of France started being afraid of the King of
England, there would be something sadly amiss in Europe. We grant you our royal protection on whichever
of our domains it will please you to choose.

BECKET. I humbly thank your Majesty. I must, however, tell you that I cannot buy this protection with any act hostile to my country.

LOUIS. You do us injury. That was understood. You may be sure we are practiced enough in the task of Kingship not to make such gross errors in our choice of spies and traitors. The King of France will ask nothing of you. But . . . There is always a but, as I'm sure you are aware, in politics.

> BECKET *looks up. The* KING *rises heavily onto his fat legs, goes to him and says familiarly:*

I am only responsible for France's interests, Becket. I really can't afford to shoulder those of Heaven. In a month or a year I can summon you back here and tell you, just as blandly, that my dealings with the King of England have taken a different turn and that I am obliged to banish you.

> *He slaps him affably on the back, his eyes sparkling with intelligence and asks, with a smile:*

I believe you have dabbled in politics too, Archbishop?

BECKET. (*Smiling*) Yes, Sire. Not so very long ago.

LOUIS. (*Jovially*) I like you very much. Mark you, had you been a French Bishop, I don't say I wouldn't have clapped you in prison myself. But in the present circumstances, you have a right to my royal protection. Do you value candor, Becket?

BECKET. Yes, Sire.

LOUIS. Then we are sure to understand each other. Do you intend to go to see the Holy Father?

BECKET. Yes, Sire, if you give me your safe conduct.

LOUIS. You shall have it. But a word in your ear—as a friend. (Keep this to yourself, won't you?—don't go and stir up trouble for me with Rome.) Beware of the

Pope. He'll sell you for thirty pieces of silver. The man needs money.

The lights dim. A curtain closes. Two small rostrums, bearing the POPE *and the* CARDINAL, *are pushed on stage, to a light musical accompaniment.*

The POPE *is a thin, fidgety little man with an atrocious Italian accent. The* CARDINAL *is swarthy, and his accent is even worse. The whole effect is a little grubby, among the gilded splendor.*

POPE. I don't agree, Zambelli! I don't agree at all! It's a very bad plan altogether. We will forfeit our honor all for 3,000 silver marks.

CARDINAL. Holy Father, there is no question of forfeiting honor, but merely of taking the sum offered by the King of England and thereby gaining time. To lose that sum and give a negative answer right away would solve neither the problems of the Curia, nor those of Thomas Becket—nor even, I am afraid, those of the higher interests of the Church. To accept the money— the sum is meager, I agree, and cannot be viewed as a factor in our decision—is merely to make a gesture of appeasement in the interests of peace in Europe. Which has always been the supreme duty of the Holy See.

POPE. (*Concerned*) If we take money from the King, I cannot possibly receive the Archbishop, who has been waiting here in Rome for a whole month for me to grant him an audience.

CARDINAL. Receive the money from the King, Very Holy Father, and receive the Archbishop too. The one will neutralize the other. The money will remove all subversive taint from the audience you will grant the Archbishop and on the other hand, the reception of the Archbishop will efface whatever taint of humiliation there may have been in accepting the money.

POPE. (*Gloomily*) I don't want to receive him at all. I

gather he is a sincere man. I am always disconcerted by people of that sort. They leave me with a bad taste in my mouth.

CARDINAL. Sincerity is a form of strategy, just like any other, Holy Father. In certain very difficult negotiations, when matters are not going ahead and the usual tactics cease to work, I have been known to use it myself. The great pitfall, of course, is if your opponent starts being sincere at the same time as you. Then the game becomes horribly confusing.

POPE. You know what they say Becket's been meaning to ask me?—in the month he's spent pacing about my antechamber?

CARDINAL. (*Innocently*) No, Holy Father.

POPE. (*Impatiently*) Zambelli! Don't play the fox with me! It was you who told me!

CARDINAL. (*Caught out*) I beg your pardon, Holy Father, I had forgotten. Or rather, as Your Holiness asked me the question, I thought you had forgotten and so I took a chance and—

POPE. (*Irritably*) Zambelli, if we start outmaneuvering each other to no purpose, we'll be here all night!

CARDINAL. (*In confusion*) Force of habit, your Holiness. Excuse me.

POPE. To ask me to relieve him of his rank and functions as Archbishop of Canterbury—that's the reason Becket is in Rome! And do you know why he wants to ask me that?

CARDINAL. (*Candidly for once*) Yes, Holy Father.

POPE. (*Irritably*) No, you do not know! It was your enemy Rapallo who told me!

CARDINAL. (*Modestly*) Yes, but I knew it just the same, because I have a spy in Rapallo's palace.

POPE. (*With a wink*) Culograti?

CARDINAL. No. Culograti is only my spy in his master's eyes. By the man I have spying on Culograti.

POPE. (*Cutting short the digression*) Becket maintains that the election of Clarendon was not a free one, that he owes his nomination solely to the royal whim and that consequently the honor of God, of which he has now decided he is the champion, does not allow him to bear this usurped title any longer. He wishes to be nothing more than an ordinary priest.

CARDINAL. (*After a moment's thought*) The man is clearly an abyss of ambition.

POPE. And yet he knows that we know that his title and functions are his only safeguard against the King's anger. I don't give much for his skin wherever he is, when he is no longer Archbishop!

CARDINAL. (*Thoughtfully*) He's playing a deep game. But I have a plan. Your Holiness will pretend to believe in his scruples. You will receive him and relieve him of his titles and functions as Primate, then, immediately after, as a reward for his zeal in defending the Church of England, you will reappoint him Archbishop, in right and due form this time. We thus avert the danger, we score a point against him—and at the same time a point against the King.

POPE. That's a dangerous game. The King has a long arm.

CARDINAL. We can cover ourselves. We will send secret letters to the English court explaining that this new nomination is a pure formality and that we herewith rescind the excommunications pronounced by Becket; on the other hand, we will inform Becket of the exist-

ence of these secret letters, swearing him to secrecy
and begging him to consider them as null and void.

POPE. (*Getting muddled*) In that case, perhaps there isn't
much point in the letters being secret?

CARDINAL. Yes, there is. Because that will allow us to ma-
neuver with each of them as if the other was ignorant
of the contents, while taking the precaution of making
it known to them both. The main thing is for them not
to know that we know they know. It's so simple a child
of twelve could grasp it!

POPE. But Archbishop or no, what are we going to do
with Becket?

CARDINAL. (*With a lighthearted wave of his hand*) We
will send him to a convent. A French convent, since
King Louis is protecting him—to the Cistercians say,
at Pontigny. The monastic rule is a strict one. It will
do that onetime dandy a world of good! Let him learn
real poverty! That will teach him to be the comforter
of the poor!

POPE. That sounds like good advice, Zambelli. Bread and
water and nocturnal prayers are an excellent remedy
for sincerity.
   He muses a moment.
The only thing that puzzles me, Zambelli, is why you
should want to give me a piece of good advice . . .
   The CARDINAL *looks a little embarrassed.*
   *The little rostra go as they came and the curtain
   opens revealing a small, bare cell, center stage.*
   BECKET *is praying before a humble wooden crucifix. Crouching in a corner, the* YOUNG MONK *is
   playing with a knife.*

BECKET. Yet it would be simple enough. Too simple perhaps. Saintliness is a temptation too. Oh, how difficult it
is to get an answer from You, Lord! I was slow in
praying to You, but I cannot believe that others, worth-

ier than I, who have spent years asking You questions,
have been better than myself at deciphering Your real
intentions. I am only a beginner and I must make mistake after mistake, as I did in my Latin translations as a
boy, when my riotous imagination made the old priest
roar with laughter. But I cannot believe that one learns
Your language as one learns any human tongue, by
hard studying, with a dictionary, a grammar and a set
of idioms. I am sure that to the hardened sinner, who
drops to his knees for the first time and murmurs Your
name, marveling, You tell him all Your secrets,
straightaway, and that he understands. I have served
You like a dilettante, surprised that I could still find
my pleasure in Your service. And for a long time I
was on my guard because of it. I could not believe this
pleasure would bring me one step nearer You. I could
not believe that the road could be a happy one. Their
hair shirts, their fasting, their bells in the small hours
summoning one to meet You, on the icy paving stones,
in the sick misery of the poor ill-treated human animal—I cannot believe that all these are anything but
safeguards for the weak. In power and in luxury, and
even in the pleasures of the flesh, I shall not cease to
speak to You, I feel this now. You are the God of
the rich man and the happy man too, Lord, and therein
lies Your profound justice. You do not turn away Your
eyes from the man who was given everything from
birth. You have not abandoned him, alone in his en-
snaring facility. And he may be Your true lost
sheep. For Your scheme of things, which we mis-
takenly call Justice, is secret and profound and You
plumb the hidden depths of poor men's puny frames as
carefully as those of Kings. And beneath those outward differences, which blind us, but which to You are
barely noticeable; beneath the diadem or the grime,
You discern the same pride, the same vanity, the same
petty, complacent preoccupation with oneself. Lord, I
am certain now that You meant to tempt me with this
hair shirt, object of so much vapid self-congratulation!
this bare cell, this solitude, this absurdly endured win-
ter-cold—and the conveniences of prayer. It would be

too easy to buy You like this, at so low a price. I shall leave this convent, where so many precautions hem You round. I shall take up the miter and the golden cope again, and the great silver cross, and I shall go back and fight in the place and with the weapons it has pleased You to give me. It has pleased You to make me Archbishop and to set me, like a solitary pawn, face to face with the King, upon the chessboard. I shall go back to my place, humbly, and let the world accuse me of pride, so that I may do what I believe is my life's work. For the rest, Your will be done.

He crosses himself.

The YOUNG MONK *is still playing with his knife. Suddenly he throws it and watches as it quivers, embedded in the floor.*

THE CURTAIN FALLS

END OF ACT THREE

ACT FOUR

The King of France's Court.

KING LOUIS *comes in, holding* BECKET *familiarly by the arm.*

LOUIS. I tell you, Becket, intrigue is an ugly thing. You keep the smell about you for ages afterwards. There is a return of good understanding between the Kingdom of England and Ourselves. Peace in that direction assures me of a great advantage in the struggle which I will shortly have to undertake against the Emperor. I must protect my rear by a truce with Henry Plantagenet, before I march towards the East. And, needless to say, you are one of the items on the King's bill of charges. I can even tell you, that apart from yourself, his demands are negligible. (*Musingly*) Curious man. England's best policy would have been to take advantage of the Emperor's aggressive intentions and close the other jaw of the trap. He is deliberately sacrificing this opportunity for the pleasure of seeing you driven out. He really hates you, doesn't he?

BECKET. (*Simply*) Sire, we loved each other and I think he cannot forgive me for preferring God to him.

LOUIS. Your King isn't doing his job properly, Archbishop. He is giving way to passion. However! He has chosen to score a point against you, instead of against me. You are on his bill, I have to pay his price and banish you. I do not do so without a certain shame. Where are you thinking of going?

BECKET. I am a shepherd who has remained too long away from his flock. I intend to go back to England. I had already made my decision before this audience with your Majesty.

LOUIS. (*Surprised*) You have a taste for martyrdom? You disappoint me. I thought you more healthy-minded.

BECKET. Would it be healthy-minded to walk the roads of Europe, and beg a refuge where my carcass would be safe? Besides, where would I be safe? I am a Primate of England. That is a rather showy label on my back. The honor of God and common sense, which for once coincide, dictate that instead of risking the knife thrust

of some hired assassin, on the highway, I should go and
have myself killed—if killed I must be—clad in my
golden cope, with my miter on my head and my silver
cross in my hand, among my flock in my own cathedral.
That place alone befits me.

    A pause.

LOUIS. I daresay you're right. (*He sighs*) Ah, what a pity
it is to be a King, sometimes, when one has the surprise
of meeting a man! You'll tell me, fortunately for me,
that men are rare. Why weren't you born on this side
of the Channel, Becket? (*He smiles*) True, you would
no doubt have been a thorn in *my* side then! The honor
of God is a very cumbersome thing.

    He muses for a moment and then says abruptly:
Who cares, I'll risk it! I like you too much. I'll indulge
in a moment's humanity. I am going to try something,
even if your master does seize on the chance to double
his bill. After all, banishing you would merely have cost
me a small slice of honor . . . I am meeting Henry in a
day or two, at La Ferté-Bernard, to seal our agreement. I shall try to persuade him to make his peace
with you. Should he agree, will you be willing to talk
with him?

BECKET. Sire, ever since we stopped seeing each other, I
have never ceased to talk to him.

    *Blackout. Prolonged blare of trumpets. The set is
    completely removed. Nothing remains but the
    cyclorama around the bare stage. A vast, arid
    plain, lashed by the wind. Trumpets again.*
    Two SENTRIES *are on stage, watching something
    in the distance.*

SENTRY. Open those eyes of yours, lad! And drink it all
in. You're new to the job, but you won't see something like this every day! This a historic meeting!

YOUNG SENTRY. I daresay, but it's perishing cold! How
long are they going to keep us hanging about?

SENTRY. We're sheltered by the wood here, but you can bet they're even colder than we are, out there in the plain.

YOUNG SENTRY. Look! They've come up to each other! I wonder what they're talking about?

SENTRY. What do you think they're talking about, mutton-head? Inquiring how things are at home? Complaining about their chilblains? The fate of the world, that's what they're arguing about! Things you and I won't ever understand. Even the words those bigwigs use— why, you wouldn't even know what they meant!

> *They go off. The lights go up.* BECKET *and the* KING, *on horseback, are alone in the middle of the plain, facing each other.*
> *Throughout the scene, the winter blizzard wails like a shrill dirge beneath their words. And during their silences, only the wind is heard.*

KING. You look older, Thomas.

BECKET. You too, Highness. Are you sure you aren't too cold?

KING. I'm frozen stiff. You love it of course! You're in your element, aren't you? And you're barefooted as well!

BECKET. (*Smiling*) That's my latest affectation.

KING. Even with these fur boots on, my chilblains are killing me. Aren't yours, or don't you have any?

BECKET. (*Gently*) Of course.

KING. (*Cackling*) You're offering them up to God, I hope, holy monk?

BECKET. (*Gravely*) I have better things to offer Him.

KING. (*With a sudden cry*) If we start straightaway, we're sure to quarrel! Let's talk about trivial things. You know my son is fourteen? He's come of age.

BECKET. Has he improved at all?

KING. He's a little idiot and sly like his mother. Becket, don't you ever marry!

BECKET. (*Smiling*) The matter has been taken out of my hands. By you, Highness! It was you who had me ordained!

KING. (*With a cry*) Let's not start yet, I tell you! Talk about something else!

BECKET. (*Lightly*) Has your Highness done much hunting lately?

KING. (*Snarling*) Yes, every day! And it doesn't amuse me any more.

BECKET. Have you any new hawks?

KING. (*Furiously*) The most expensive on the market! But they don't fly straight.

BECKET. And your horses?

KING. The Sultan sent me four superb stallions for the tenth anniversary of my reign. But they throw everyone! Nobody has managed to mount one of them, yet!

BECKET. (*Smiling*) I must see what I can do about that some day.

KING. They'll throw you too! And we'll see your buttocks under your robe! At least, I hope so, or everything would be too dismal.

BECKET. (*After a pause*) Do you know what I miss most, Sire? The horses.

KING. And the women?

BECKET. (*Simply*) I've forgotten.

KING. You hypocrite. You turned into a hypocrite when you became a priest. (*Abruptly*) Did you love Gwendolen?

BECKET. I've forgotten her too.

KING. You did love her! That's the only way I can account for it.

BECKET. (*Gravely*) No, my prince, in my soul and conscience, I did not love her.

KING. Then you never loved anything, that's worse! (*Churlishly*) Why are you calling me your prince, like in the old days?

BECKET. (*Gently*) Because you have remained my prince.

KING. (*Crying out*) Then why are you doing me harm?

BECKET. (*Gently*) Let's talk about something else.

KING. Well, what? I'm cold.

BECKET. I always told you, my prince, that one must fight the cold with the cold's own weapons. Strip naked and splash yourself with cold water every morning.

KING. I used to when you were there to force me into it. I never wash now. I stink. I grew a beard at one time. Did you know?

BECKET. (*Smiling*) Yes. I had a hearty laugh over it.

KING. I cut it off because it itched.
    He cries out suddenly, like a lost child:
Becket, I'm bored!

BECKET. (*Gravely*) My prince. I do so wish I could help
    you.

KING. Then what are you waiting for? You can see I'm
    dying for it!

BECKET. (*Quietly*) I'm waiting for the honor of God and
    the honor of the King to become one.

KING. You'll wait a long time then!

BECKET. Yes. I'm afraid I will.
    A pause. Only the wind is heard.

KING. (*Suddenly*) If we've nothing more to say to each
    other, we might as well go and get warm!

BECKET. We have everything to say to each other, my
    prince. The opportunity may not occur again.

KING. Make haste, then. Or there'll be two frozen statues
    on this plain making their peace in a frozen eternity! I
    am your King, Becket! And so long as we are on this
    earth you owe me the first move! I'm prepared to for-
    get a lot of things but not the fact that I am King. You
    yourself taught me that.

BECKET. (*Gravely*) Never forget it, my prince. Even
    against God. You have a different task to do. You
    have to steer the ship.

KING. And you—what do you have to do?

BECKET. Resist you with all my might, when you steer
    against the wind.

KING. Do you expect the wind to be behind me, Becket?

No such luck! That's the fairy-tale navigation! God on the King's side? That's never happened yet! Yes, once in a century, at the time of the Crusades, when all Christendom shouts "It's God's will!" And even then! You know as well as I do what private greeds a Crusade covers up, in nine cases out of ten. The rest of the time, it's a head-on wind. And there must be somebody to keep the watch!

BECKET. And somebody else to cope with the absurd wind—and with God. The tasks have been shared out, once and for all. The pity of it is that it should have been between us two, my prince—who were friends.

KING. (*Crossly.*) The King of France—I still don't know what he hopes to gain by it—preached at me for three whole days for me to make my peace with you. What good would it do you to provoke me beyond endurance?

BECKET. None.

KING. You know that I am the King, and that I must act like a King! What do you expect of me? Are you hoping I'll weaken?

BECKET. No. That would prostrate me.

KING. Do you hope to conquer me by force then?

BECKET. You are the strong one.

KING. To win me round?

BECKET. No. Not that either. It is not for me to win you round. I have only to say no to you.

KING. But you must be logical, Becket!

BECKET. No, that isn't necessary, my Liege. We must

only do—absurdly—what we have been given to do—
right to the end.

KING. Yet I know you well enough, God knows. Ten years
we spent together, little Saxon! At the hunt, at the
whorehouse, at war; carousing all night long the two of
us; in the same girl's bed, sometimes . . . and at work in
the Council Chamber too. Absurdly. That word isn't
like you.

BECKET. Perhaps. I am no longer like myself.

KING. (*Derisively*) Have you been touched by grace?

BECKET. (*Gravely*) Not by the one you think. I am not
worthy of it.

KING. Did you feel the Saxon in you coming out, despite
Papa's good collaborator's sentiments?

BECKET. No. Not that either.

KING. What then?

BECKET. I felt for the first time that I was being entrusted with something, that's all—there in that empty
cathedral, somewhere in France, that day when you
ordered me to take up this burden. I was a man without honor. And suddenly I found it—one I never
imagined would ever become mine—the honor of God.
A frail, incomprehensible honor, vulnerable as a boy-
King fleeing from danger.

KING. (*Roughly*) Suppose we talked a little more pre-
cisely, Becket, with words I understand? Otherwise
we'll be here all night. I'm cold. And the others are
waiting for us on the fringes of this plain.

BECKET. I am being precise.

KING. I'm an idiot then! Talk to me like an idiot! That's

an order. Will you lift the excommunication which you pronounced on William of Aynsford and others of my liegemen?

BECKET. No, Sire, because that is the only weapon I have to defend this child, who was given, naked, into my care.

KING. Will you agree to the twelve proposals which my Bishops have accepted in your absence at Northampton, and notably to forego the much-abused protection of Saxon clerics who get themselves tonsured to escape land bondage?

BECKET. No, Sire. My role is to defend my sheep. And they are my sheep.
    A pause.
Nor will I concede that the Bishops should forego the right to appoint priests in their own dioceses, nor that churchmen should be subject to any but the Church's jurisdiction. These are my duties as a pastor—which it is not for me to relinquish. But I shall agree to the nine other articles in a spirit of peace, and because I know that you must remain King—in all save the honor of God.
    A pause.

KING. (*Coldly*) Very well. I will help you defend your God, since that is your new vocation, in memory of the companion you once were to me—in all save the honor of the Realm. You may come back to England, Thomas.

BECKET. Thank you, my prince. I meant to go back in any case and give myself up to your power, for on this earth, you are my King. And in all that concerns this earth, I owe you obedience.
    A pause.

KING. (*Ill at ease*) Well, let's go back now. We've finished. I'm cold.

BECKET. (*Dully*) I feel cold too, now.
      *Another pause. They look at each other. The
      wind howls.*

KING. (*Suddenly*) You never loved me, did you, Becket?

BECKET. In so far as I was capable of love, yes, my
   prince, I did.

KING. Did you start to love God?
      He cries out:
   You mule! Can't you ever answer a simple question?

BECKET. (*Quietly*) I started to love the honor of God.

KING. (*Somberly*) Come back to England. I give you my
   royal peace. May you find yours. And may you not dis-
   cover you were wrong about yourself. This is the last
   time I shall come begging to you.
      He cries out:
   I should never have seen you again! It hurts too much.
      His whole body is suddenly shaken by a sob.

BECKET. (*Goes nearer to him; moved*) My prince—

KING. (*Yelling*) No! No pity! It's dirty. Stand away from
   me! Go back to England! It's too cold out here!
      BECKET *turns his horse and moves nearer to the*
      KING.

BECKET. (*Gravely*) Farewell, my prince. Will you give
   me the kiss of peace?

KING. No! I can't bear to come near you! I can't bear to
   look at you! Later! Later! When it doesn't hurt any
   more!

BECKET. I shall set sail tomorrow. Farewell, my prince. I
   know I shall never see you again.

KING. (*His face twisted with hatred*) How dare you say

that to me after I gave you my royal word? Do you
take me for a traitor?

> BECKET *looks at him gravely for a second longer,*
> *with a sort of pity in his eyes. Then he slowly*
> *turns his horse and rides away. The wind howls.*

KING. Thomas!

> *But* BECKET *has not heard. The* KING *does not*
> *call a second time. He spurs his horse and gal-*
> *lops off in the other direction. The lights fade.*
> *The wind howls.*
> *The lights change. Red curtains fall.* BECKET'S
> *whistled march is heard off stage during the scene*
> *change.*
> *The curtains open. Royal music. King Henry's*
> *palace somewhere in France. The two* QUEENS,
> *the* BARONS *and Henry's* SON *are standing around*
> *the dinner table, waiting. The* KING, *his eyes*
> *gleaming maliciously, looks at them and then ex-*
> *claims:*

KING. Today, gentlemen, I shall not be the first to sit
down! (*To his* SON, *with a comic bow*) You are the
King, Sir. The honor belongs to you. Take the high
chair. Today I shall wait on *you!*

QUEEN MOTHER. (*With slight irritation*) My son!

KING. I know what I'm doing, Madam! (*With a sudden*
shout) Go on, you great loon, look sharp! You're the
King, but you're as stupid as ever!

> *The boy flinches to avoid the blow he was ex-*
> *pecting and goes to sit in the* KING'S *chair, sly*
> *and rather ill at ease.*

Take your places, gentlemen! I shall remain standing.
Barons of England, here is your second King. For the
good of our vast domains, a kingly colleague had become a necessity. Reviving an ancient custom, we have
decided to have our successor crowned during our
lifetime and to share our responsibilities with him. We

ask you now to give him your homage and to honor him with the same title as Ourself.

He makes a sign. Two SERVANTS *have brought in a haunch of venison on a silver charger. The* KING *serves his* SON.

YOUNG QUEEN. (*To her* SON) Sit up straight! And try to eat properly for once, now that you've been raised to glory!

KING. (*Grunting as he serves him*) He hasn't the face for it! He's a little slyboots and dim-witted at that. However, he'll be your King in good earnest one day, so you may as well get used to him. Besides, it's the best I had to offer.

QUEEN MOTHER. (*Indignantly*) Really, my son! This game is unworthy of you and of us. You insisted on it—against my advice—at least play it with dignity!

KING. (*Rounding on her in fury*) I'll play the games that amuse me, Madam, and I'll play them the way I choose! This mummery, gentlemen, which is, incidentally, without any importance at all—(if your new King fidgets, let me know, I'll give him a good kick up his train)—will at the very least have the appreciable result of showing our new friend, the Archbishop, that we can do without him. If there was one ancient privilege the Primacy clung to, tooth and nail, it was its exclusive right to anoint and consecrate the Kings of this realm. Well, it will be that old toad the Archbishop of York —with letters from the Pope authorizing him to do so—I paid the price!—who, tomorrow, will crown our son in the cathedral! What a joke that's going to be!

He roars with laughter amid the general silence. What a tremendous, marvelous joke! I'd give anything to see that Archbishop's face when he has to swallow that! (*To his* SON) Get down from there, you imbecile! Go back to the bottom of the table and take your victuals with you! You aren't officially crowned until tomorrow.

The boy picks up his plate and goes back to his place, casting a cowed, smoldering look at his father.

(*Watching him, says jovially*) What a look! Filial sentiments are a fine thing to see, gentlemen! You'd like to be the real King, wouldn't you, you young pig? You'd like that number III after your name, eh, with Papa good and stiff under his catafalque! You'll have to wait a bit! Papa is well. Papa is very well indeed!

QUEEN MOTHER. My son, God knows I criticized your attempts at reconciliation with that wretch, who has done us nothing but harm . . . God knows I understand your hatred of him! But do not let it drag you into making a gesture you will regret, merely for the sake of wounding his pride. Henry is still a child. But you were not much older when you insisted on reigning by yourself, and in opposition to me. Ambitious self-seekers—and there is never any scarcity of those around Princes—can advise him, raise a faction against you and avail themselves of this hasty coronation to divide the Kingdom! Think it over, there is still time.

KING. We are still alive, Madam, and in control! And nothing can equal my pleasure in imagining my proud friend Becket's face when he sees the fundamental privilege of the Primacy whisked from under his nose! I let him cheat me out of one or two articles the other day, but I had something up my sleeve for him!

QUEEN MOTHER. Henry! I bore the weight of state affairs longer than you ever have. I have been your Queen and I am your mother. You are answerable for the interests of a great Kingdom, not for your moods. You already gave far too much away to the King of France, at La Ferté-Bernard. It is England you must think of, not your hatred—or disappointed love—for that man.

KING. (*In a fury*) Disappointed love—disappointed love? What gives you the right, Madam, to meddle in my loves and hates?

QUEEN MOTHER. You have a rancor against the man which is neither healthy nor manly. The King your father dealt with his enemies faster and more summarily than that. He had them killed and said no more about it. If Thomas Becket were a faithless woman whom you still hankered after, you would act no differently. Sweet Jesu, tear him out of your heart once and for all!

She bawls suddenly:

Oh, if I were a man!

KING. (*Grinning*) Thanks be to God, Madam, he gave you dugs. Which I never personally benefited from. I suckled a peasant girl.

QUEEN MOTHER. (*Acidly*) That is no doubt why you have remained so lumpish, my son.

YOUNG QUEEN. And haven't I a say in the matter? I tolerated your mistresses, Sir, but do you expect me to tolerate everything? Have you ever stopped to think what kind of woman I am? I am tired of having my life encumbered with this man. Becket! Always Becket! Nobody ever talks about anything else here! He was almost less of a hindrance when you loved him. I am a woman. I am your wife and your Queen. I refuse to be treated like this! I shall complain to my father, the Duke of Aquitaine! I shall complain to my uncle, the Emperor! I shall complain to all the Kings of Europe, my cousins! I shall complain to God!

KING. (*Shouting rather vulgarly*) I should start with God! Be off to your private chapel, Madam, and see if He's at home.

He turns to his mother, fuming.

And you, the other Madam, away to your chamber with your secret councilors and go and spin your webs! Get out, both of you! I can't stand the sight of you! I retch with boredom whenever I set eyes on you! And young Henry III too! Go on, get out!

He chases him out with kicks, yelling:

Here's my royal foot in your royal buttocks! And to
the devil with my whole family, if he'll have you! Get
out, all of you! Get out! Get out! Get out!

The QUEENS *scurry out, with a great rustling of
silks. He turns to the* BARONS *who all stand watching him, terror-stricken.*

(*More calmly*) Let us drink, gentlemen. That's about
all one can do in your company. Let us get drunk, like
men, all night; until we roll under the table, in vomit
and oblivion.

He fills their glasses and beckons them closer.

Ah, my four idiots! My faithful hounds! It's warm beside you, like being in a stable. Good sweat! Comfortable nothingness!

He taps their skulls.

Not the least little glimmer inside to spoil the fun.
And to think that before he came I was like you! A
good fat machine for belching after drink, for pissing,
for mounting girls and punching heads. What the devil
did you put into it, Becket, to stop the wheels from
going round? (*Suddenly to the* 2ND BARON) Tell me,
do you think sometimes, Baron?

2ND BARON. Never, Sire. Thinking has never agreed with
an Englishman. It's unhealthy. Besides, a gentleman has
better things to do.

KING. (*Sitting beside them, suddenly quite calm*) Drink
up, gentlemen. That's always been considered a
healthy thing to do.

He fills the goblets.

Has Becket landed? I'm told the sea has been too rough
to cross these last few days.

1ST BARON. (*Somberly*) He has landed, Sire, despite the
sea.

KING. Where?

1ST BARON. On a deserted stretch of coast, near Sand-
wich.

KING. So God did not choose to drown him?

1ST BARON. No.

KING. (*He asks in his sly, brutish way*) Was nobody there waiting for him? There must be one or two men in England whom he can't call his friends!

1ST BARON. Yes. Gervase, Duke of Kent, Regnouf de Broc and Regnault de Garenne were waiting for him. Gervase had said that if he dared to land he'd cut off his head with his own hands. But the native Englishmen from all the coastal towns had armed themselves to form an escort for the Archbishop. And the Dean of Oxford went to meet the Barons and charged them not to cause bloodshed and make you look a traitor, seeing that you had given the Archbishop a safe conduct.

KING. (*Soberly*) Yes, I gave him a safe conduct.

1ST BARON. All along the road to Canterbury, the peasants, the artisans and the small shopkeepers came out to meet him, cheering him and escorting him from village to village. Not a single rich man, not a single Norman, showed his face.

KING. Only the Saxons?

1ST BARON. Poor people armed with makeshift shields and rusty lances. Riffraff. Swarms of them though, all camping around Canterbury, to protect him. (*Gloomily*) Who would have thought there were so many people in England!
The KING *has remained prostrate without uttering a word. Now he suddenly jumps up and roars:*

KING. A miserable wretch who ate my bread! A man I raised up from nothing! A Saxon! A man loved! (*Shouting like a madman*) I loved him! Yes, I loved him! And I believe I still do! Enough, O God! Enough! Stop, stop, O God, I've had enough!
He flings himself down on the couch, sobbing hysterically; tearing at the horsehair mattress

with his teeth, and eating it. The BARONS, *stupefied, go nearer to him.*

1ST BARON. (*Timidly*) Your Highness . . .

KING. (*Moaning, with his head buried in the mattress*) I can do nothing! Nothing! I'm as limp and useless as a girl! So long as he's alive, I'll never be able to do a thing. I tremble before him astonished. And I am the King! (*With a sudden cry*) Will no one rid me of him? A priest! A priest who jeers at me and does me injury! Are there none but cowards like myself around me? Are there no men left in England? Oh, my heart! My heart is beating too fast to bear!

> *He lies, still as death on the torn mattress. The four* BARONS *stand around speechless. Suddenly, on a percussion instrument, there rises a rhythmic beating, a sort of muffled tom-tom which is at first only the agitated heartbeats of the* KING, *but which swells and grows more insistent. The four* BARONS *look at each other. Then they straighten, buckle their sword belts, pick up their helmets and go slowly out, leaving the* KING *alone with the muffled rhythm of the heartbeats, which will continue until the murder. The* KING *lies there prostrate, among the upturned benches, in the deserted hall. A torch splutters and goes out. He sits up, looks around, sees they have gone and suddenly realizes why. A wild, lost look comes into his eyes. A moment's pause then he collapses on the bed with a long broken moan.*

KING. O my Thomas!

> *A second torch goes out. Total darkness. Only the steady throb of the heartbeats is heard. A dim light. The forest of pillars again. Canterbury Cathedral. Upstage a small altar, with three steps leading up to it, half screened by a grill. In a corner downstage* BECKET, *and the* YOUNG MONK, *who is helping him on with his vestments. Nearby, on a stool, the Archbishop's miter. The tall silver cross is leaning against a pillar.*

BECKET. I must look my best today. Make haste.
The MONK *fumbles with the vestments. The muffled tom-tom is heard distantly at first, then closer.*

MONK. It's difficult with all those little laces. It wants a girl's hands.

BECKET. (*Softly*) A man's hands are better, today. Never mind the laces. The alb, quickly. And the stole. And then the cope.

MONK. (*Conscientiously*) If it's worth doing it's worth doing well.

BECKET. You're quite right. If it's worth doing it's worth doing well. Do up all the little laces, every one of them. God will give us time.
A pause. The boy struggles manfully on, putting out his tongue in concentration. The throbbing grows louder.
(*Smiling*) Don't pull your tongue out like that!
He watches the boy as he works away.

MONK. (*Sweating but content*) There. That's all done. But I'd rather have cleaned out our pigsty at home! It's not half such hard work!

BECKET. Now the alb.
A pause.
Were you fond of your pigs?

MONK. (*His eyes lighting up*) Yes, I was.

BECKET. At my father's house, we had some pigs too, when I was a child. (*Smiling*) We're two rough lads from Hastings, you and I! Give me the chasuble.
BECKET *kisses the chasuble and slips it over his head. He looks at the boy and says gently:*
Do you miss your knife?

MONK. Yes.

Pause.
Will it be today?

BECKET. (*Gravely*) I think so, my son. Are you afraid?

MONK. Oh, no. Not if we have time to fight. All I want is
the chance to strike a few blows first; so I shan't have
done nothing but receive them all my life. If I can kill
one Norman first—just one, I don't want much—one
for one, that will seem fair and right enough to me.

BECKET. (*With a kindly smile*) Are you so very set on
killing one?

MONK. One for one. After that, I don't much care if I
am just a little grain of sand in the machine. Because
I know that by putting more and more grains of sand
in the machine, one day it will come grinding to a stop.

BECKET. (*Gently*) And on that day, what then?

MONK. We'll set a fine, new, well-oiled machine in the
place of the old one and this time we'll put the Normans into it instead.
      He asks, quite without irony:
That's what justice means, isn't it?
      BECKET *smiles and does not answer him.*

BECKET. Fetch me the miter.
      He says quietly, as the boy fetches it:
O Lord, You forbade Peter to strike a blow in the
Garden of Olives. But I shall not deprive him of that
joy. He has had too few joys in his short span on
earth. (*To the boy*) Now give me my silver cross. I
must hold it.

MONK. (*Passing it to him*) Lord, it's heavy! A good
swipe with that and they'd feel it! My word, I wish I
could have it!

BECKET. (*Stroking his hair*) Lucky little Saxon! This

black world will have been in order to the end, for you.

He straightens, grave once more.

There. I'm ready, all adorned for Your festivities, Lord. Do not, in this interval of waiting, let one last doubt enter my soul.

During this scene, the throbbing has grown louder. Now it mingles with a loud knocking on the door. A PRIEST *runs in wildly.*

PRIEST. Your Grace! There are four armed men outside! They say they must see you on behalf of the King. I've barricaded the door but they're breaking it in! They've got hatchets! Quickly! You must go into the back of the church and have the choir gates closed! They're strong enough, they'll hold!

BECKET. (*Calmly*) It is time for Vespers, William. Does one close the choir gates during Vespers? I never heard of such a thing.

PRIEST. (*Nonplused*) I know, but . . .

BECKET. Everything must be the way it should be. The choir gates will remain open. Come, boy, let us go up to the altar. This is no place to be.

He goes toward the altar, followed by the YOUNG MONK. *A great crash. The door has given way. The four* BARONS *come in, in their helmets. They fling down their hatchets and draw their swords.* BECKET *turns to face them, grave and calm, at the foot of the altar. They stop a moment, uncertain and disconcerted; four statues, huge and threatening. The tom-tom has stopped. There is nothing now but a heavy silence.* BECKET *says simply:*

Here it comes. The supreme folly. This is its hour.

He holds their eyes. They dare not move. He says coldly:

One does not enter armed into God's house. What do you want?

1ST BARON. (*Thickly*) Your death.

A pause.

2ND BARON. (*Thickly*) You bring shame to the King. Flee the country or you're a dead man.

BECKET. (*Softly*) It is time for the service.

>*He turns to the altar and faces the tall crucifix without paying any further attention to them. The throbbing starts again, muffled. The four men close in like automata. The YOUNG MONK suddenly leaps forward brandishing the heavy silver cross in order to protect BECKET, but one of the BARONS swings his sword and fells him to the ground. BECKET murmurs, as if in reproach:*

Not even one! It would have given him so much pleasure, Lord. (*With a sudden cry*) Oh how difficult You make it all! And how heavy Your honor is to bear!

>*He adds, very quietly:*

Poor Henry.

>*The four men hurl themselves onto him. He falls at the first blow. They hack at his body, grunting like woodcutters. The PRIEST has fled with a long scream, which echoes in the empty cathedral. Blackout.*

>*On the same spot. The KING, naked, on bended knees at BECKET's tomb, as in the first scene. Four MONKS are whipping him with ropes, almost duplicating the gestures of the BARONS as they killed BECKET.*

KING. (*Crying out*) Are you satisfied now, Becket? Does this settle our account? Has the honor of God been washed clean?

>*The four MONKS finish beating him, then kneel down and bow their heads. The KING mutters— one feels it is part of the ceremony:*

Thank you. Yes, yes, of course, it was agreed, I forgive you. Many thanks.

>*The PAGE comes forward with a vast cloak, which the KING wraps around himself. The BARONS surround the KING and help him to dress, while the BISHOPS and the CLERGY, forming a procession, move away solemnly upstage to the strains of the*

organ. The KING *dresses hurriedly, with evident bad temper, aided by his* BARONS. *He grimaces ill-humoredly and growls:*

The pigs! The Norman Bishops just went through the motions, but those little Saxon monks—my word, they had their money's worth!

A BARON *comes in. A joyful peal of bells is heard.*

BARON. Sire, the operation has been successful! The Saxon mob is yelling with enthusiasm outside the cathedral, acclaiming your Majesty's name in the same breath as Becket's! If the Saxons are on our side now, Prince Henry's followers look as though they have definitely lost the day.

KING. (*With a touch of hypocritical majesty beneath his slightly loutish manner*) The honor of God, gentlemen, is a very good thing, and taken all in all, one gains by having it on one's side. Thomas Becket, who was our friend, used to say so. England will owe her ultimate victory over chaos to him, and it is our wish that, henceforward, he should be honored and prayed to in this Kingdom as a saint. Come, gentlemen. We will determine, tonight, in Council, what posthumous honors to render him and what punishment to deal out to his murderers.

1ST BARON. (*Imperturbably*) Sire, they are unknown.

KING. (*Impenetrably*) Our justice will seek them out, Baron, and you will be specially entrusted with this inquiry, so that no one will be in any doubt as to our Royal desire to defend the honor of God and the memory of our friend from this day forward.

The organ swells triumphantly, mingled with the sound of the bells and the cheering of the crowds as they file out.

CURTAIN